PRESCHOOL SIGHT WORDS ACTIVITY BOOK

THIS BOOK BELONGS TO

_____

_____

_____

_____

READ, WRITE COLOR, AND LEARN

Flash Cards

Laminate or glue/tape onto index cards or cardstock paper to make them sturdy. Use with your child to practice the sight words used in this book.

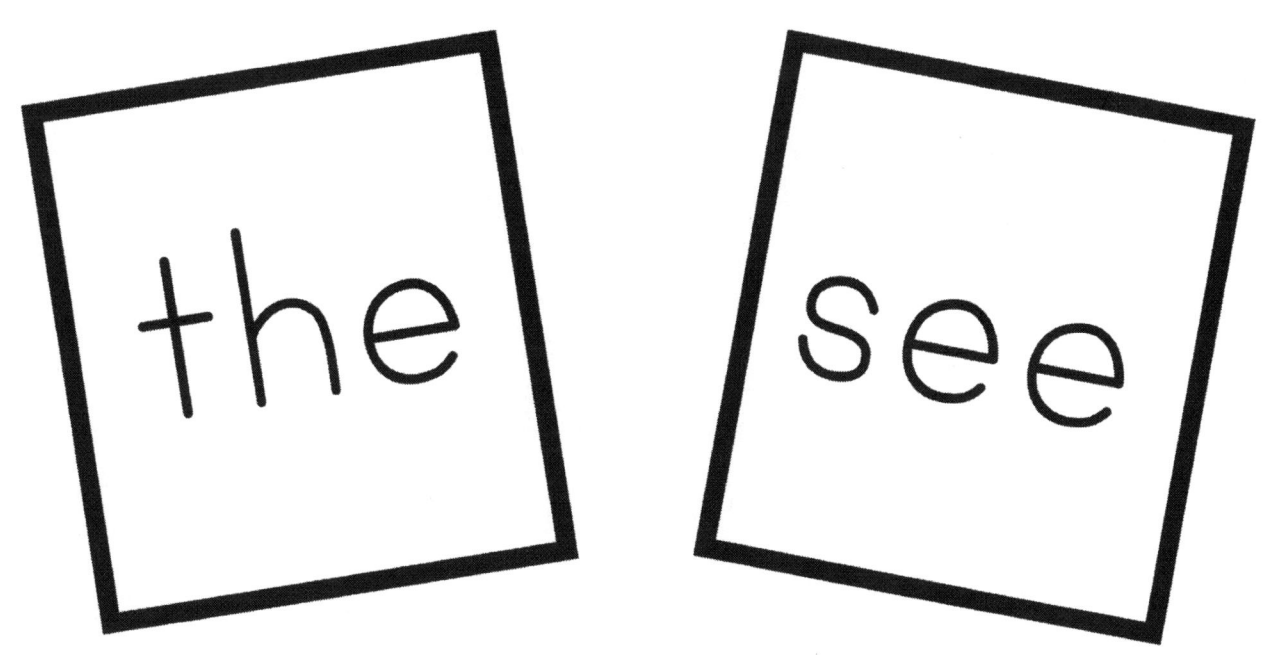

the	see
and	can

come	for
find	go

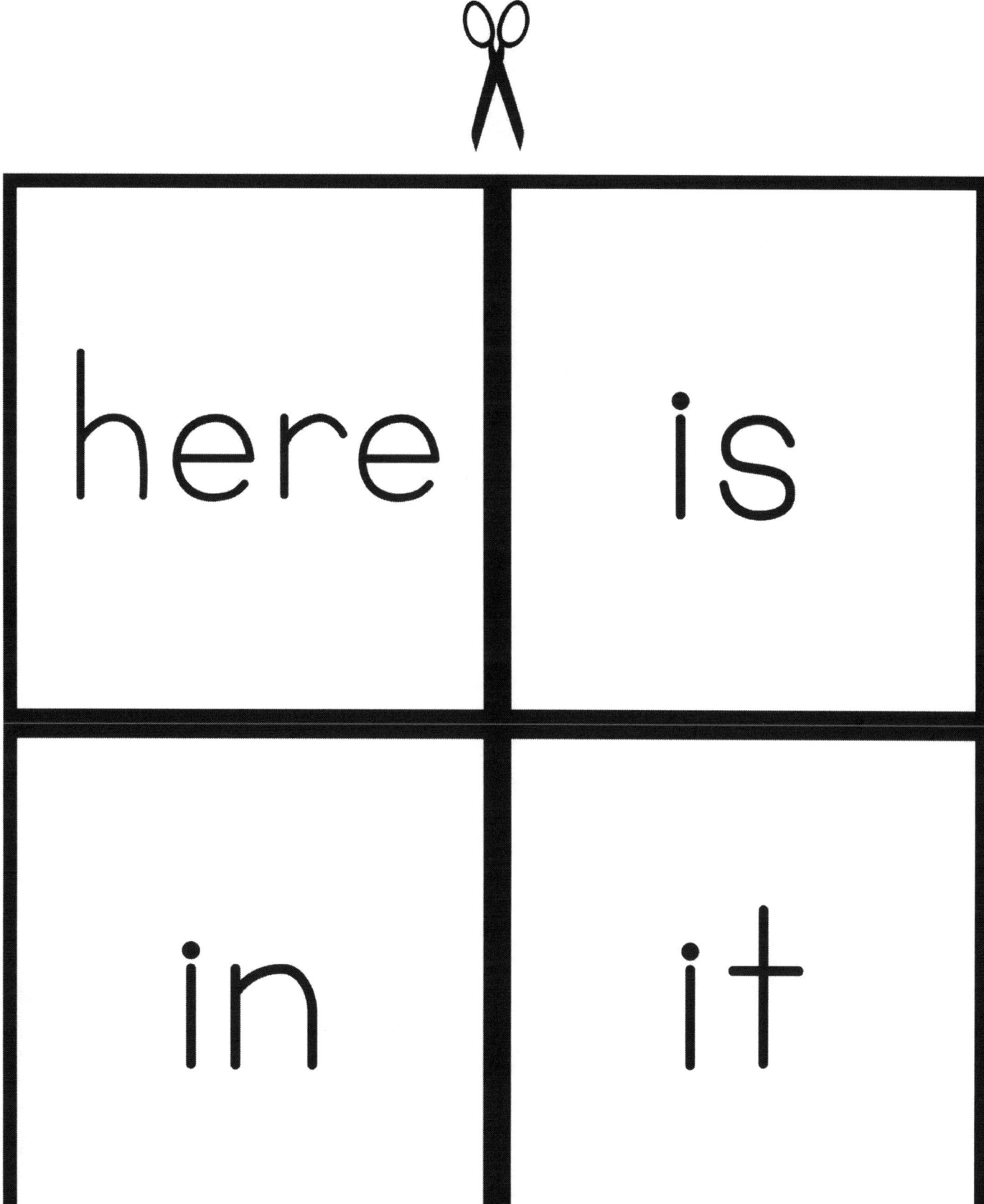

not	said
to	we

you	where
little	look

help	make
big	play

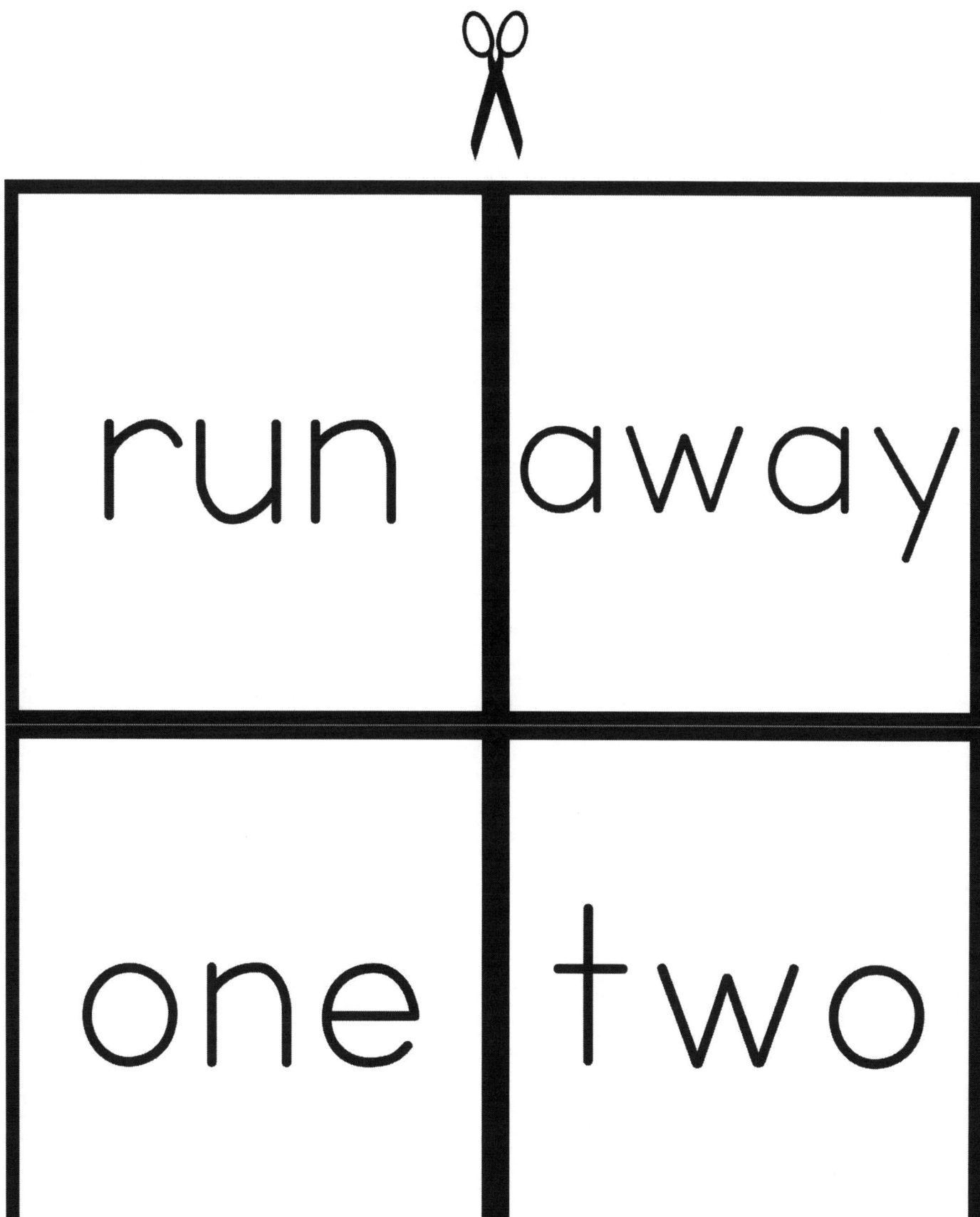

three	blue
red	yellow

jump	funny
add word here	add word here

Sight Word List

The following are the 38 high frequency preschool words used in this book:

the	it	away	one
see	big	little	two
and	look	jump	three
can	you	not	red
come	we	up	blue
for	run	play	yellow
go	help	make	
find	my	me	
here	down	funny	
in	said	to	
is	where		

Say the letters and color:

the

Read and Circle:

the the the

Trace:

the the the

Write:

th t

Say the letters and color:

Read and Circle:

see see see

Trace:

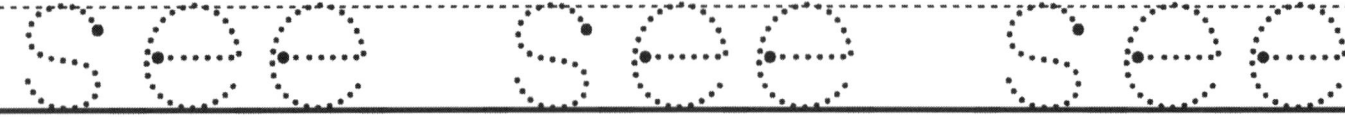

Write:

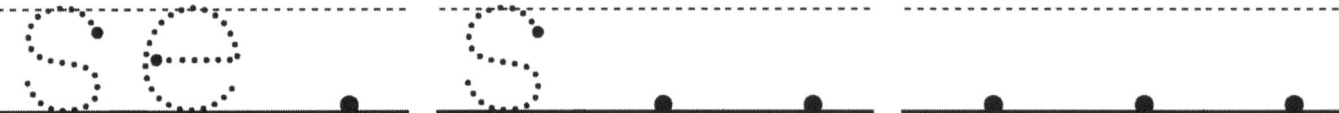

see

Read:

I see a car.

Circle:

I see a car.

Trace:

I see a car.

Write:

I _____ a car.

Say the letters and color:

Read and Circle:

and and and

Trace:

Write:

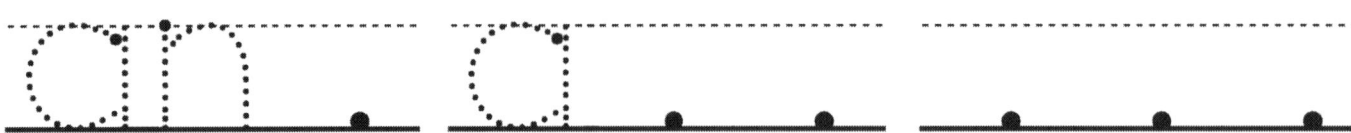

Say the letters and color:

Read and Circle:

can can can

Trace:

can can can

Write:

ca c

can

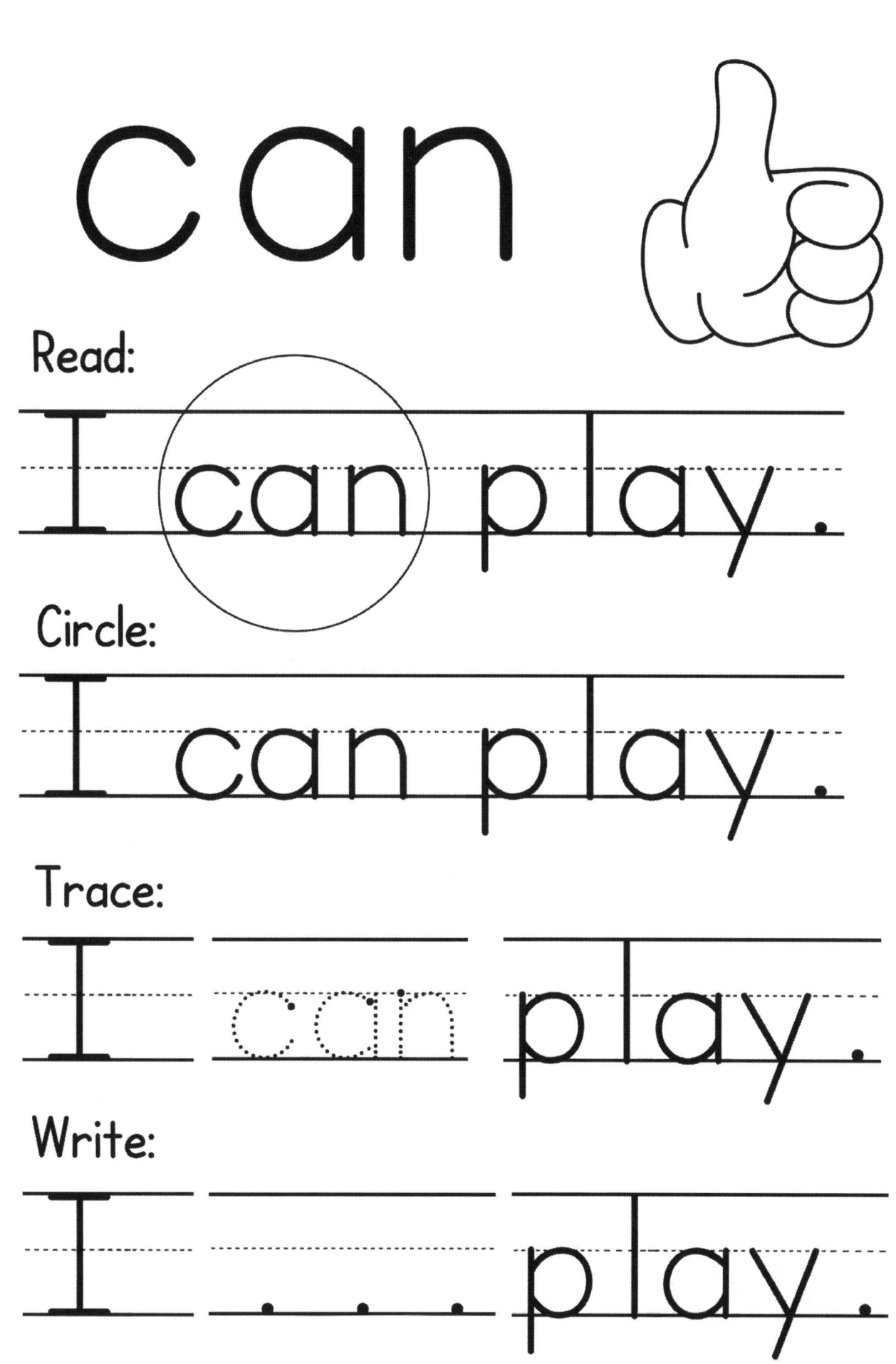

Read:

I can play.

Circle:

I can play.

Trace:

I can play.

Write:

I ..... play.

Review 1

Words learned:

the see and can

Trace the words:

the see and can

Write the words:

t.... s.... a.... c....

Find the words:

the
see
and
can

I	C	W	J	R
F	A	I	T	F
A	N	D	H	Z
M	S	E	E	E
X	W	V	E	K

Review 1

Circle the sight words in the sentences and trace the sentences:

the see and can

I like the dog.

I see a car.

I eat and drink.

I can play.

Say the letters and color: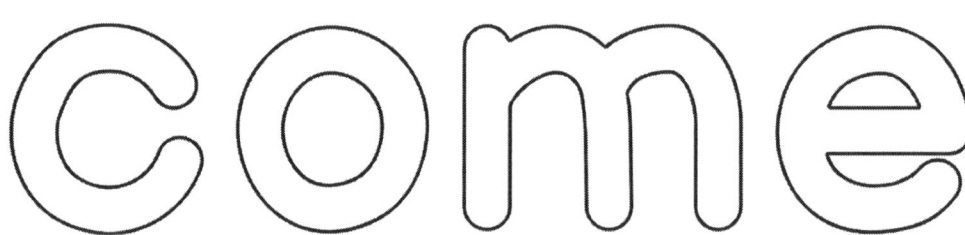

Read and Circle:

come come come

Trace:

come come come

Write:

co c

come

Read:

Come play with me.

Circle:

Come play with me.

Trace:

Come play with me.

Write:

_ _ _ _ play with me.

Say the letters and color: **for**

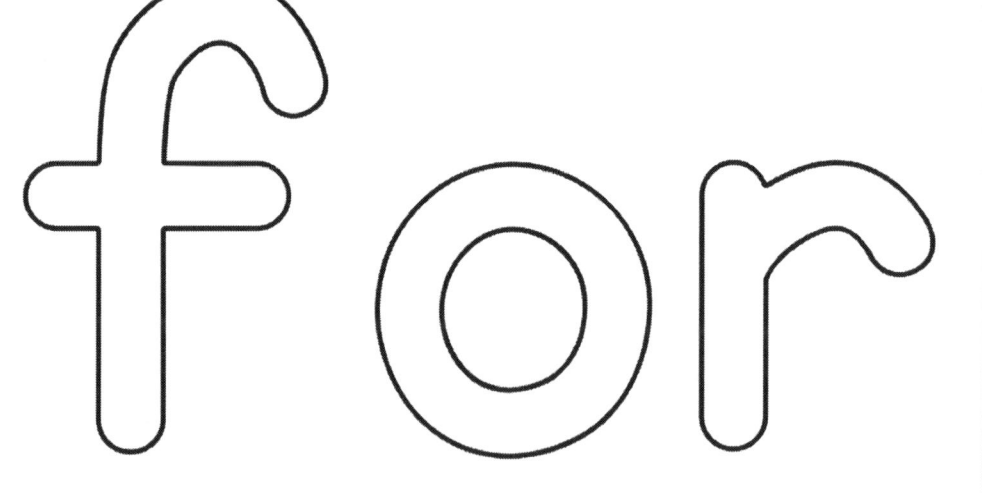

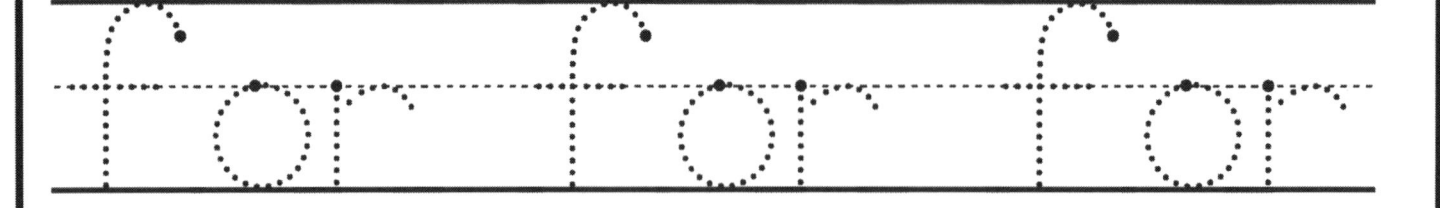

Read and Circle:

for for for

Trace:

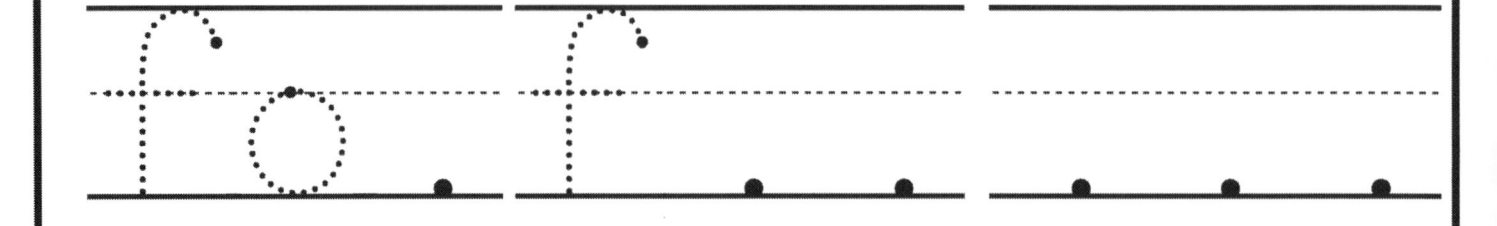

for for for

Write:

fo f

for

Read:

This is (for) you.

Circle:

This is for you.

Trace:

This is for you.

Write:

This is _____ you.

Say the letters and color:

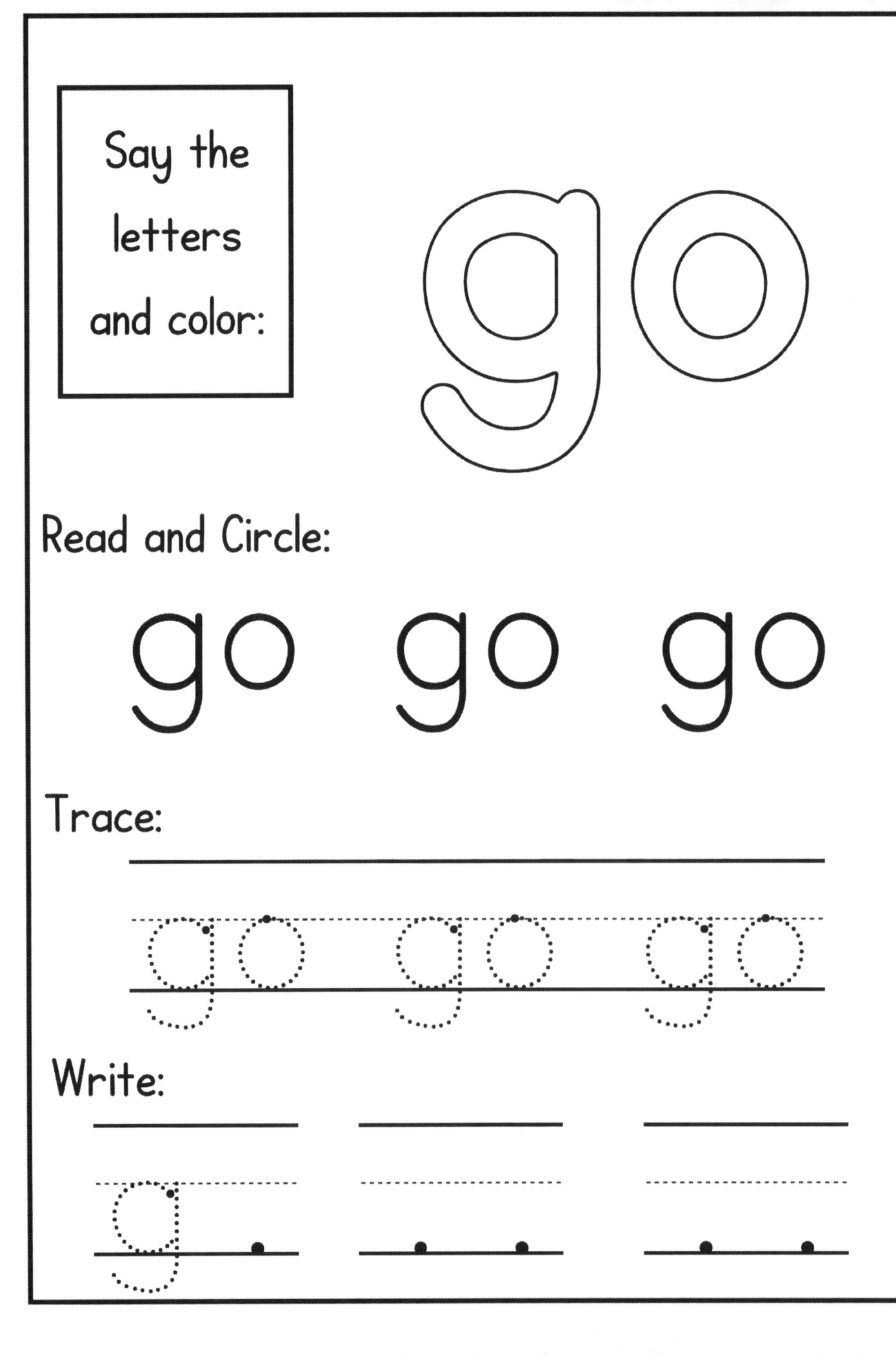

go

Read and Circle:

go go go

Trace:

go go go

Write:

g

go

Read:

I go to school.

Circle:

I go to school.

Trace:

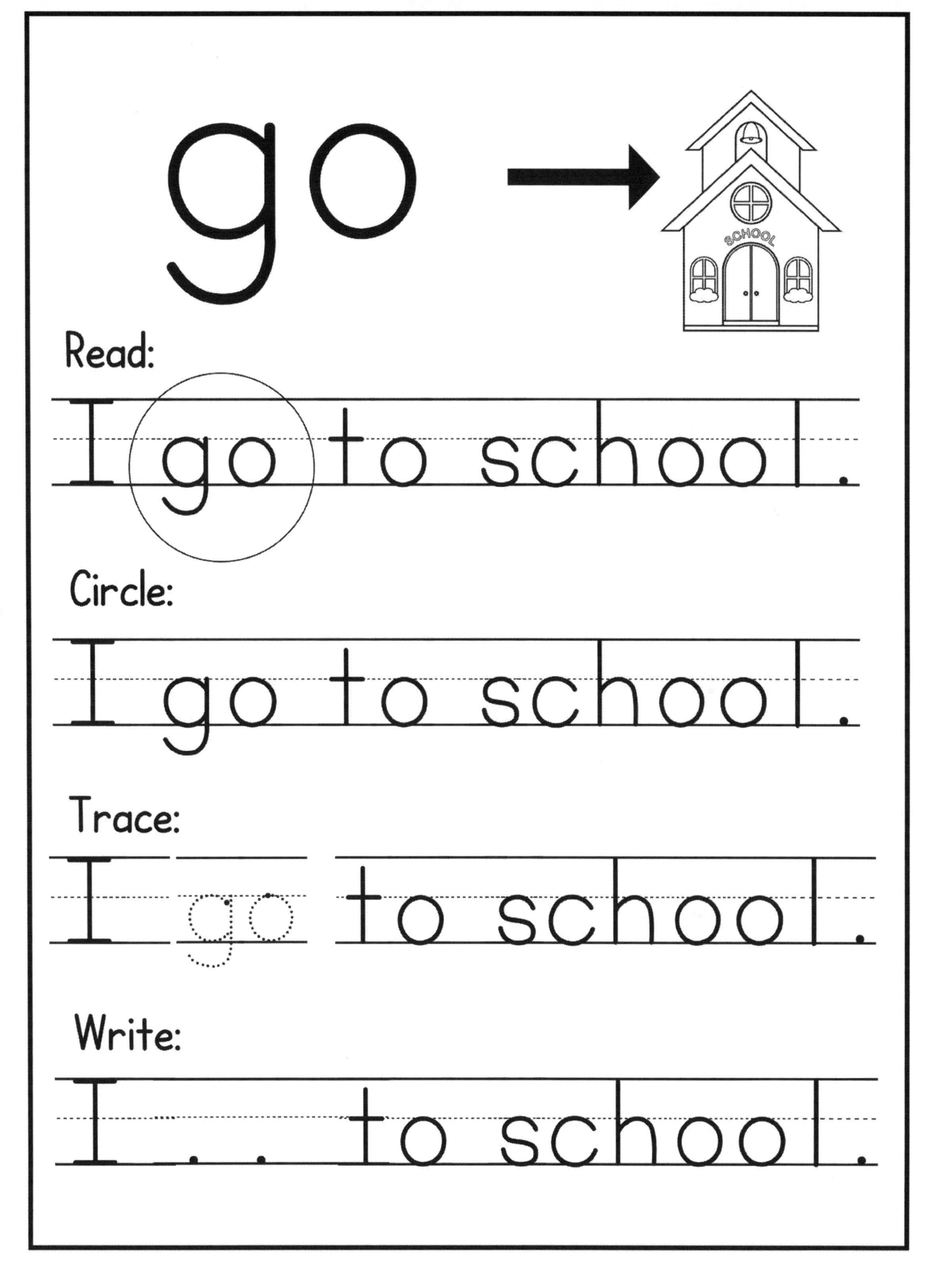

I go to school.

Write:

I ___ to school.

Say the letters and color:

find

Read and Circle:

find find find

Trace:

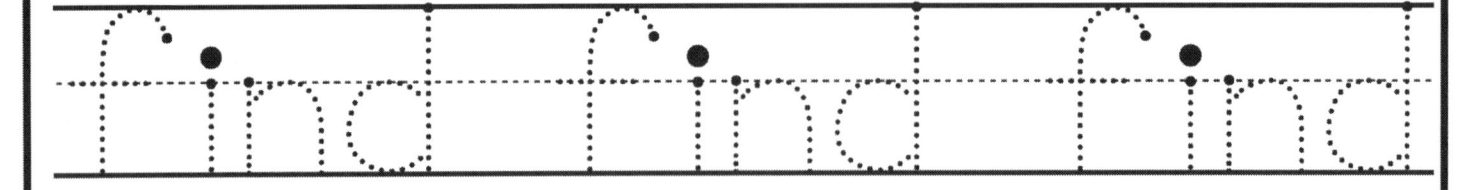

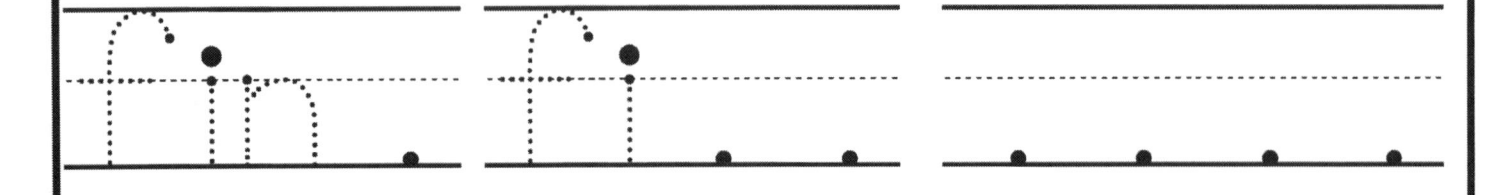

find find find

Write:

fin fi

find

Read:

Can you (find) me ?

Circle:

Can you find me ?

Trace:

Can you find me ?

Write:

Can you _____ me ?

Review 2

Words learned:

come for go find

Trace the words:

come for go find

Write the words:

c....   f....   g.   f....

Find the words:

| come |
| for |
| go |
| find |

U	F	W	F	F
C	O	M	E	I
P	R	F	W	N
H	U	G	B	D
A	Q	M	O	D

Review 2

Circle the sight words in the sentences and trace the sentences:

come for go find

Come play with me.

This is for you.

I go to school.

Can you find me?

Say the letters and color:

here

Read and Circle:

here here here

Trace:

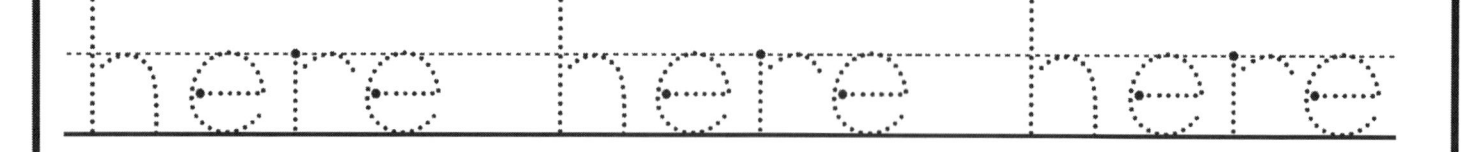

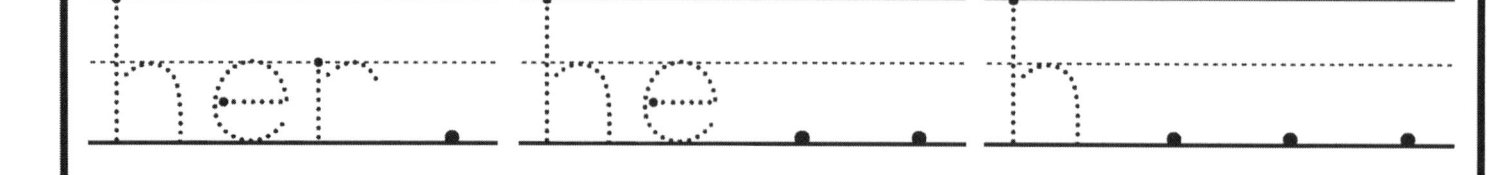

here here here

Write:

her he h

here

Read:

The toy is here.

Circle:

The toy is here.

Trace:

The toy is here.

Write:

The toy is ____.

Say the letters and color:

in

Read and Circle:

in in in

Trace:

in in in

Write:

i

in

Read:

A cat goes (in) a box.

Circle:

A cat goes in a box.

Trace:

A cat goes in a box.

Write:

A cat goes ___ a box.

Say the letters and color:

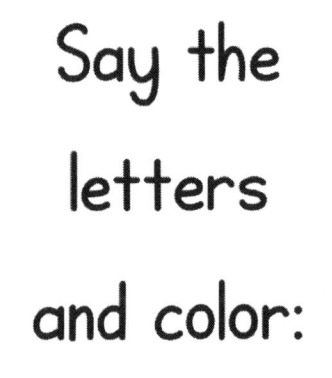

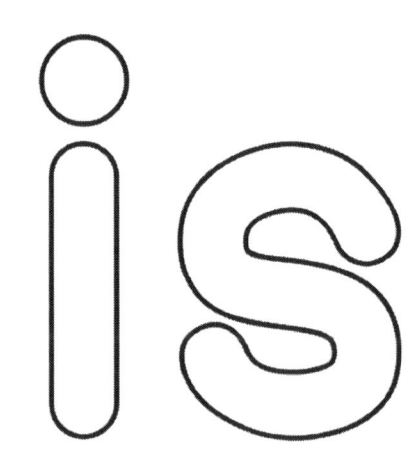

is

Read and Circle:

is   is   is

Trace:

is   is   is

Write:

is

Read:

The ball (is) big.

Circle:

The ball is big.

Trace:

The ball is big.

Write:

The ball ... big.

Say the letters and color: it

Read and Circle:

it it it

Trace:

Write:

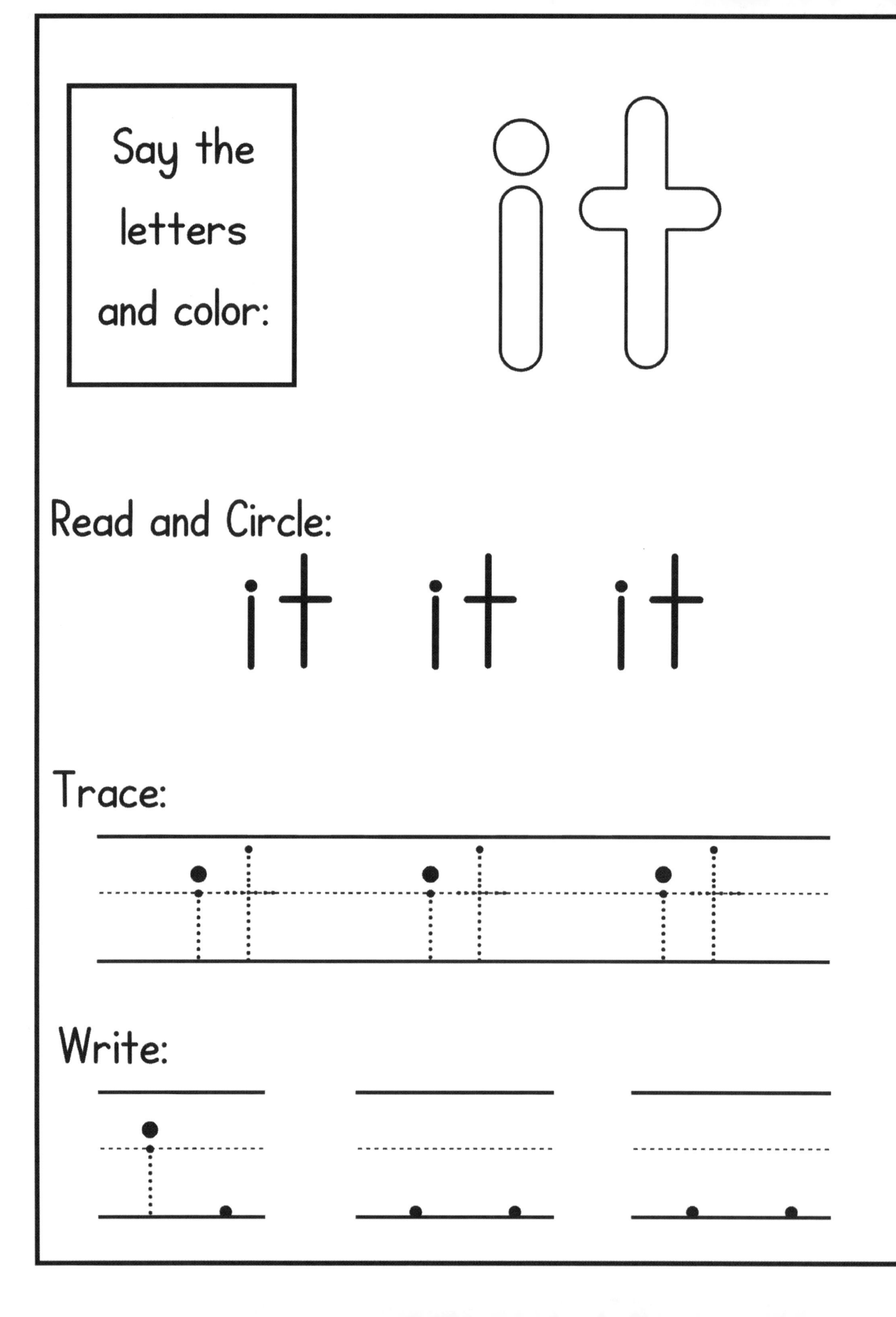

it

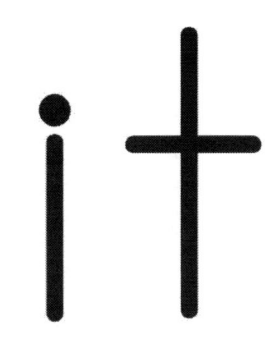

Read:

Let me have (it).

Circle:

Let me have it.

Trace:

Let me have it.

Write:

Let me have ___.

Review 3

Words learned:

here in is it

Trace the words:

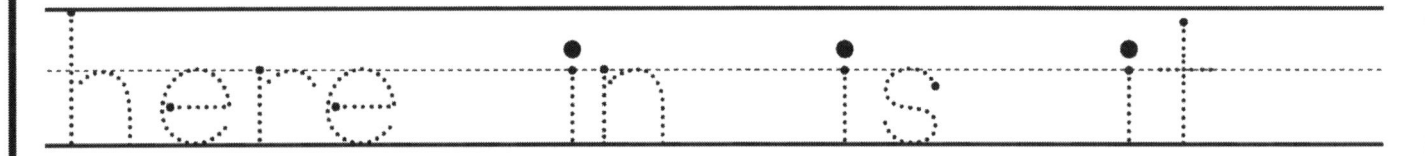

here in is it

Write the words:

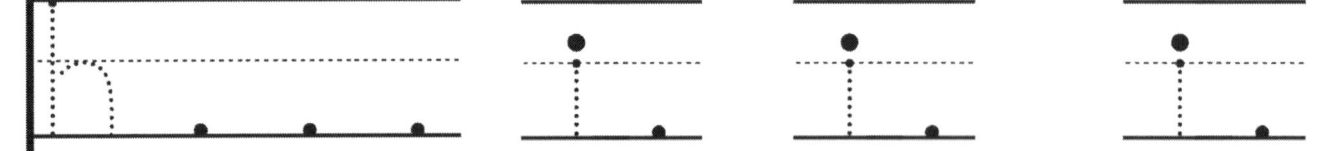

h_ _ _   i_   i_   i_

Find the words:

here
is
in
it

L	U	P	B	Z
E	J	T	Q	B
J	H	E	R	E
V	S	I	S	I
U	C	T	N	T

Review 3

Circle the sight words in the sentences and trace the sentences:

here in is it

The toy is here.

A cat goes in a box.

The ball is big.

Let me have it.

Say the letters and color:

big

Read and Circle:

big big big

Trace:

big big big

Write:

bi b

big

Read:

The fish is (big).

Circle:

The fish is big.

Trace:

The fish is big.

Write:

The fish is ___.

Say the letters and color: **look**

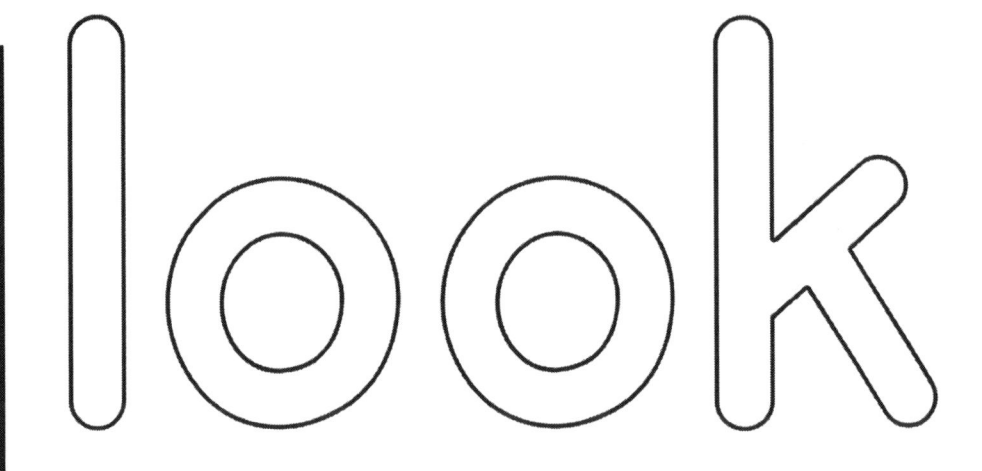

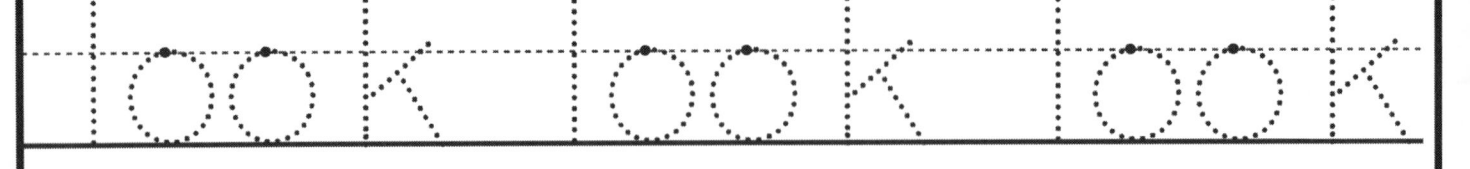

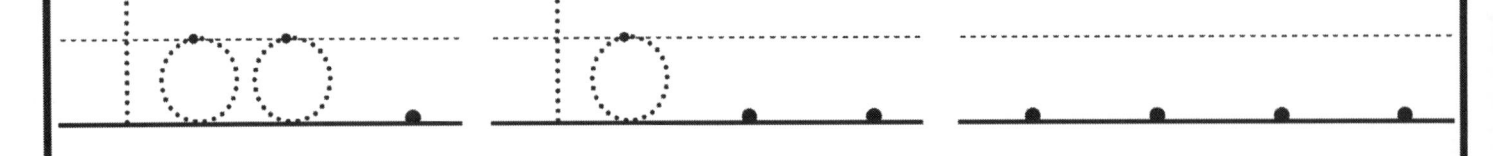

Read and Circle:
look look look

Trace:
look look look

Write:
look lo

look

Read:

Look in a book.

Circle:

Look at a book.

Trace:

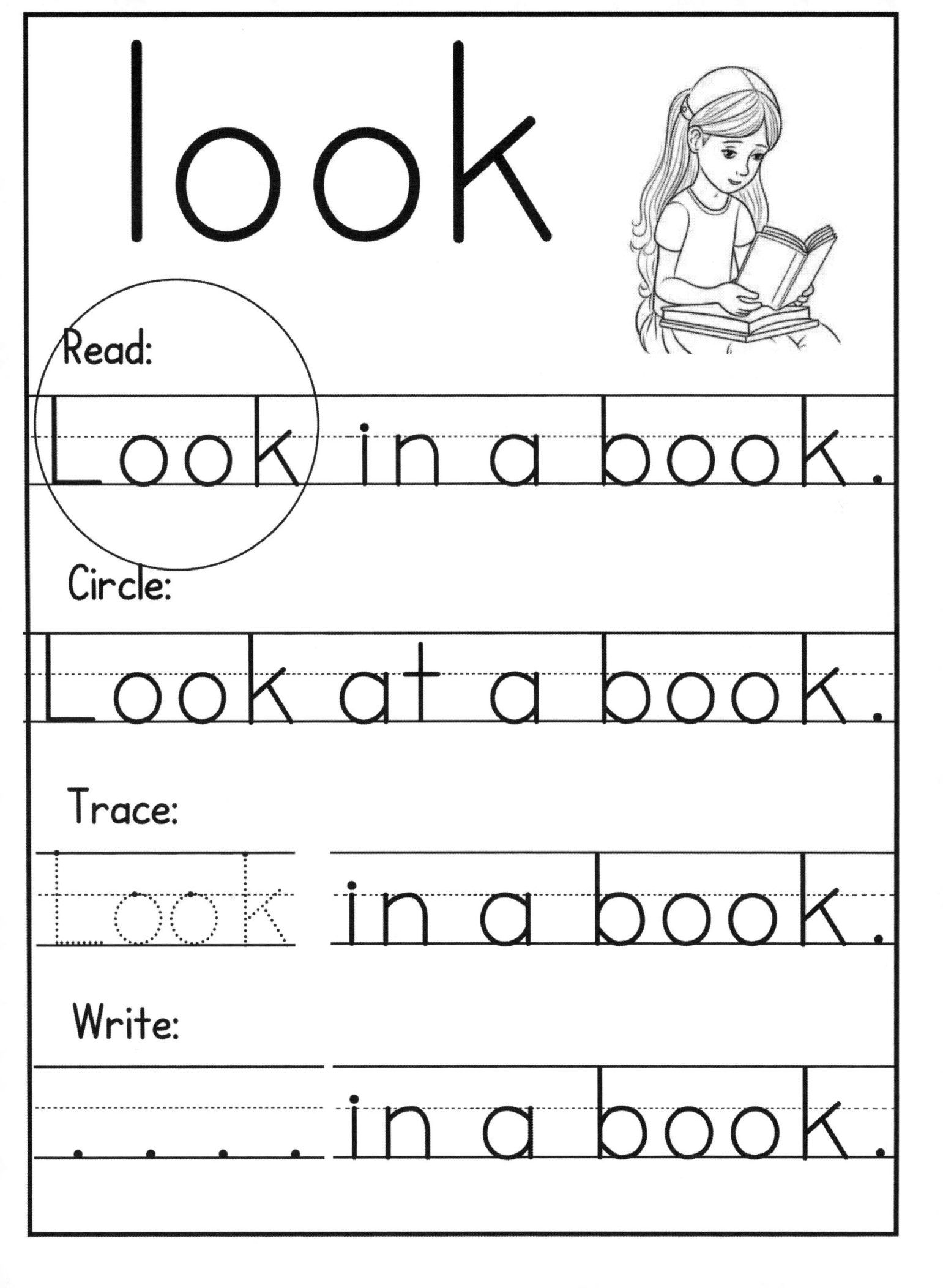

Look in a book.

Write:

_____ in a book.

Say the letters and color:

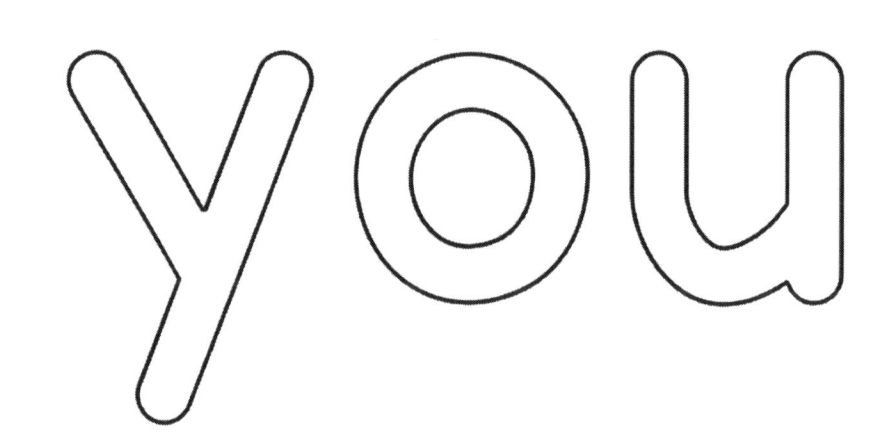

you

Read and Circle:

you you you

Trace:

you you you

Write:

yo y

you

Read:

This is for (you.)

Circle:

This is for you.

Trace:

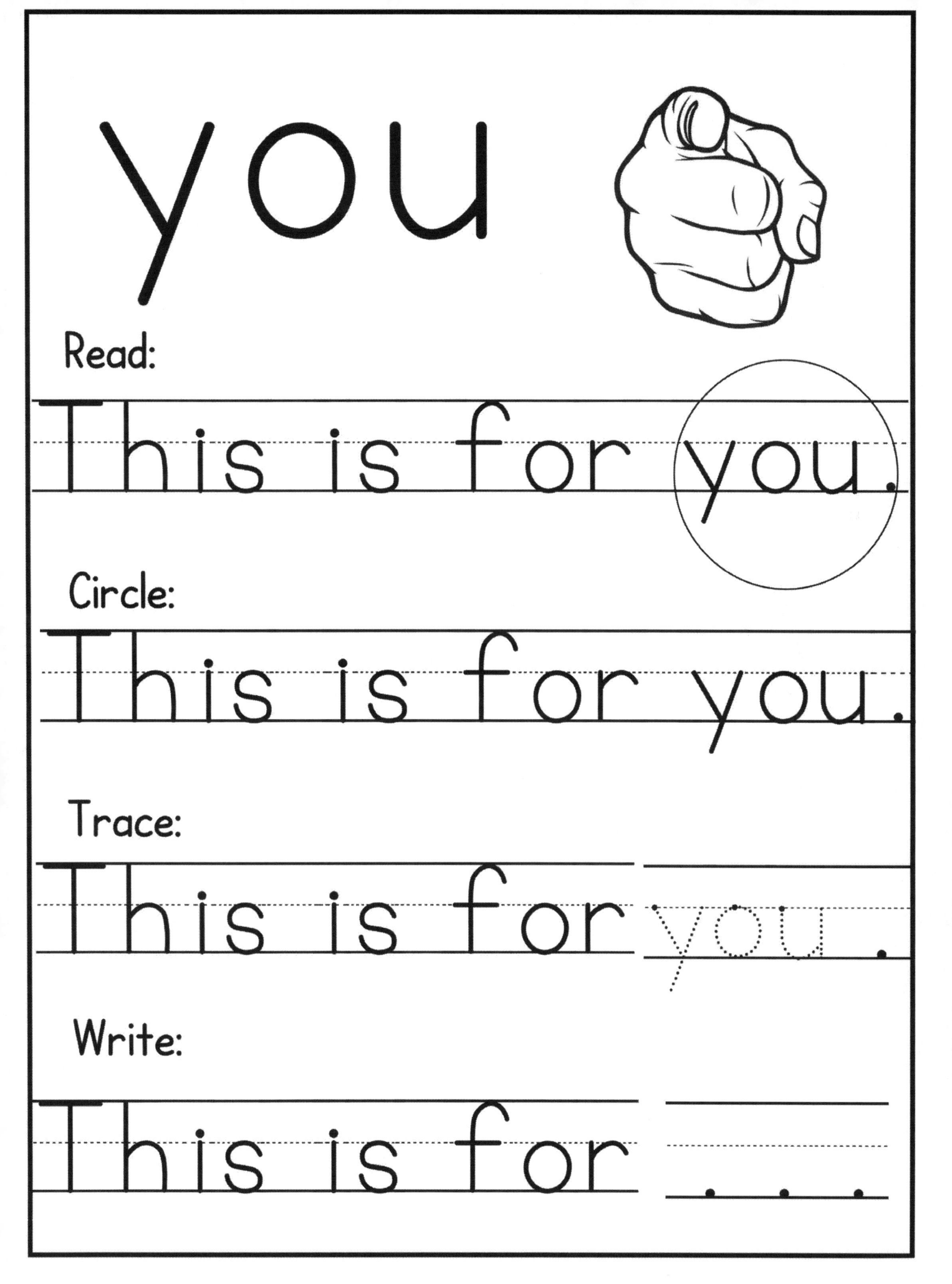

This is for you.

Write:

This is for ___.

Say the letters and color: **we**

Read and Circle:

we we we

Trace:

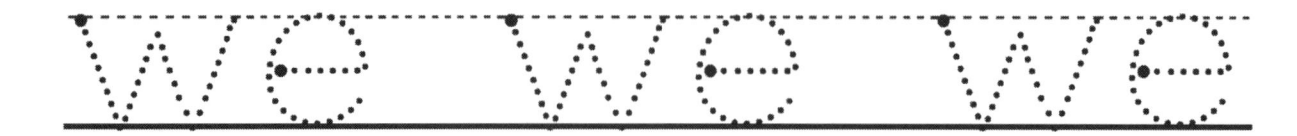

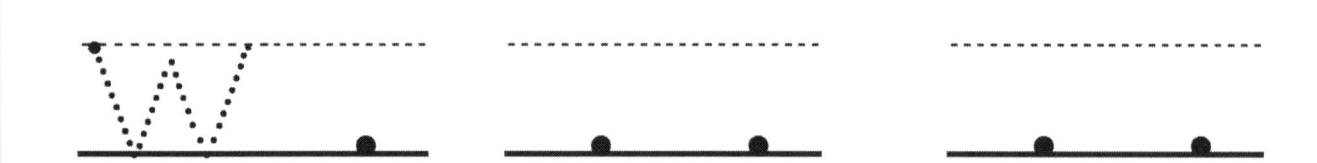

we we we

Write:

w

we

Read:

We are friends.

Circle:

We are friends.

Trace:

We are friends.

Write:

___ are friends.

Review 4

Words learned:

big look you we

Trace the words:

big look you we

Write the words:

b_ _ l_ _ _ y_ _ w_ _

Find the words:

big
look
you
we

M	K	B	I	G
Z	Y	V	F	X
L	O	O	K	R
O	Y	W	U	F
P	J	S	E	B

Review 4

Circle the sight words in the sentences and trace the sentences:

big look you we

The fish is big.

Look in a book.

This is for you.

We are friends.

Say the letters and color: run

Read and Circle:

run run run

Trace:

run run run

Write:

run

run

Read:

He can run fast.

Circle:

He can run fast.

Trace:

He can run fast.

Write:

He can ____ fast.

Say the letters and color: **help**

Read and Circle:

help help help

Trace:

help help help

Write:

he h

help

Read:

Please help me.

Circle:

Please help me.

Trace:

Please help me.

Write:

Please _____ me.

Say the letters and color:

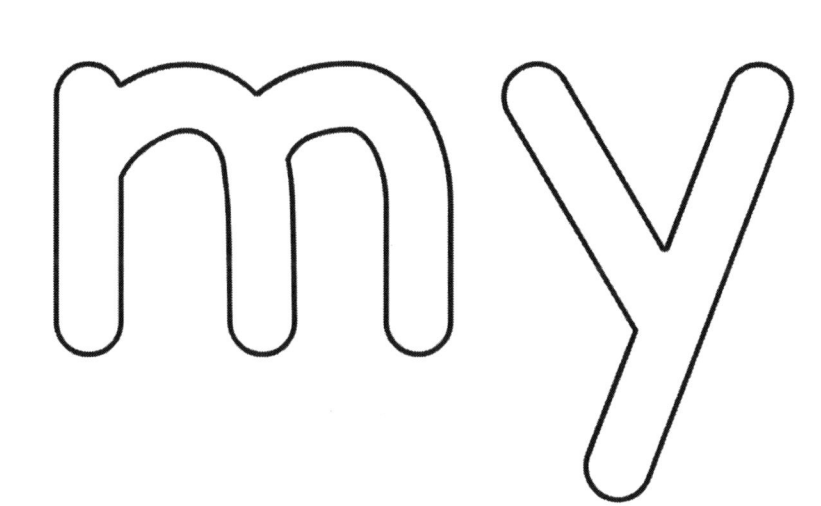

my

Read and Circle:

my my my

Trace:

my my my

Write:

m

my

Read:

This is (my) friend.

Circle:

This is my friend.

Trace:

This is my friend.

Write:

This is ___ friend.

Say the letters and color: **down**

Read and Circle:
down down down

Trace:
down down down

Write:
do do

down ⬇

Read:

My hat fell down.

Circle:

My hat fell down.

Trace:

My hat fell down.

Write:

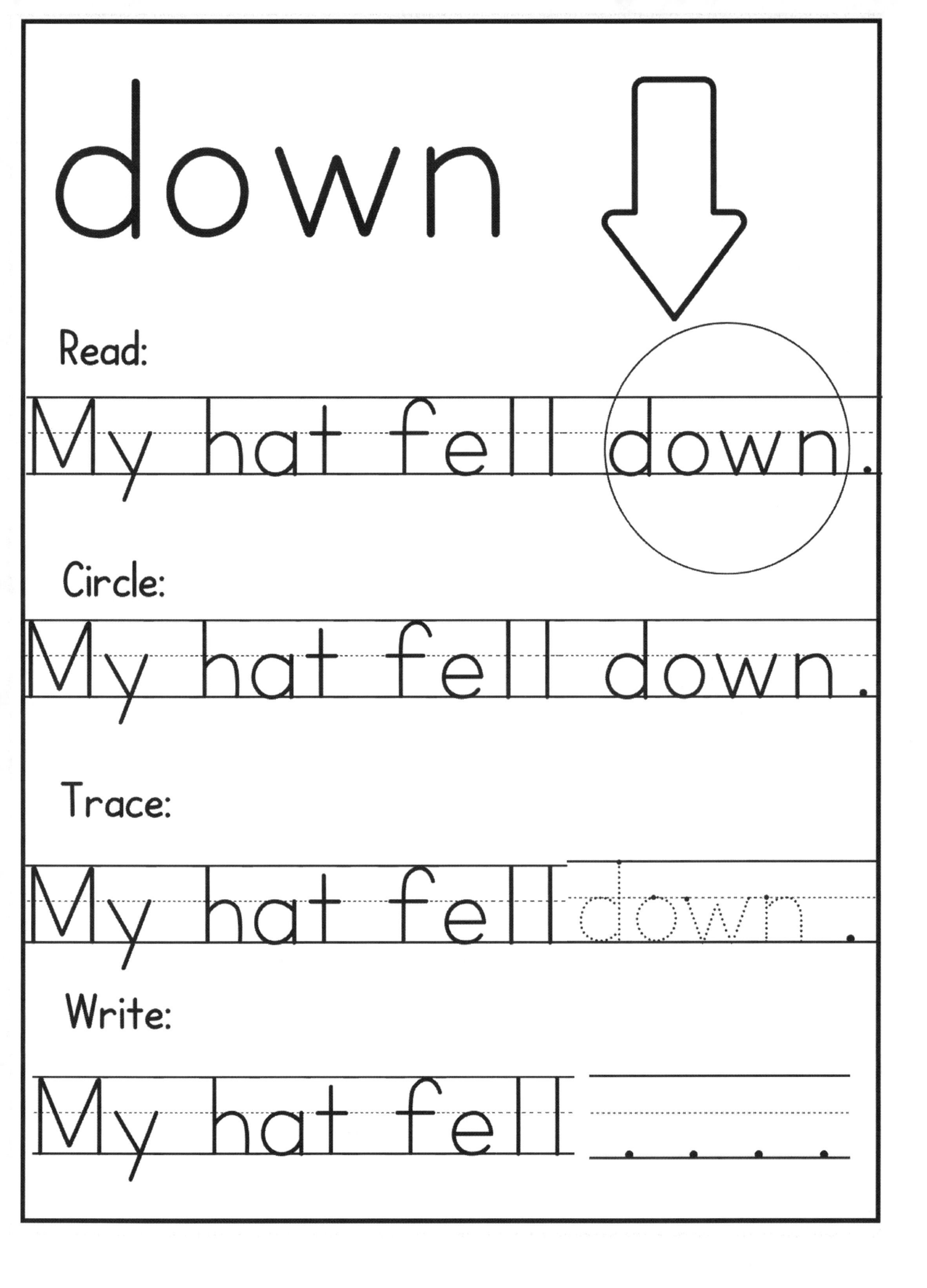

My hat fell _____.

Review 5

Words learned:

run help my down

Trace the words:

run help my down

Write the words:

r___ h___ m_ d___

Find the words:

run
help
my
down

H H L X M
C B E I Y
R U N L D
D O W N P
E V J H U

Review 5

Circle the sight words in the sentences and trace the sentences:

big look you we

He can run fast.

Please help me.

This is my friend.

My hat fell down.

Say the letters and color: **said**

Read and Circle:

said said said

Trace:

said said said

Write:

said s

said

Read:

The boy (said) hi.

Circle:

The boy said hi.

Trace:

The boy said hi.

Write:

The boy _____ hi.

Say the letters and color: **where**

Read and Circle:

where where

Trace:

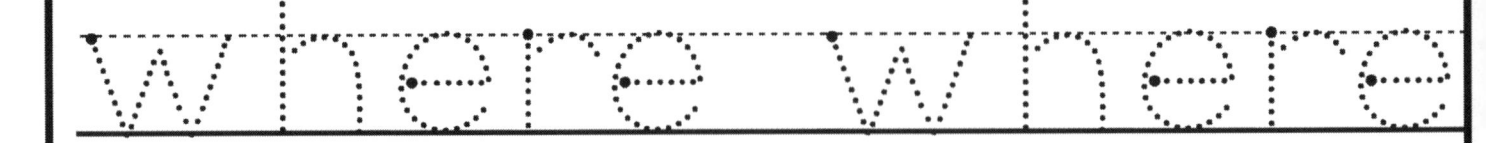

where where

Write:

wh

where

Read:

Where did you go ?

Circle:

Where did you go ?

Trace:

Where did you go ?

Write:

W...... did you go ?

Say the letters and color: **away**

Read and Circle:

away away away

Trace:

away away away

Write:

aw.. a....

away

Read:

I said go (away).

Circle:

I said go away.

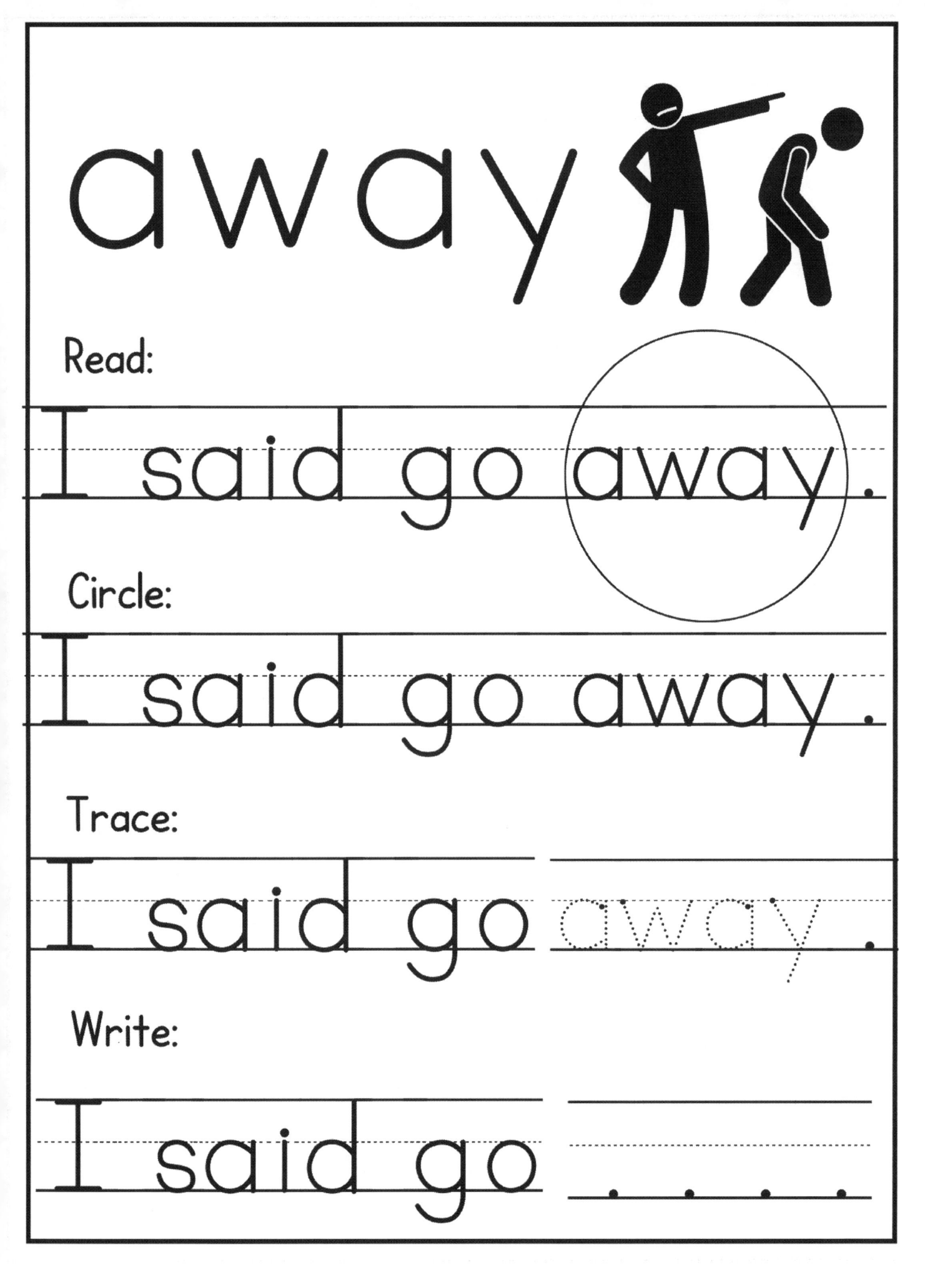

Trace:

I said go away.

Write:

I said go _____.

Say the letters and color: **little**

Read and Circle:
little little little

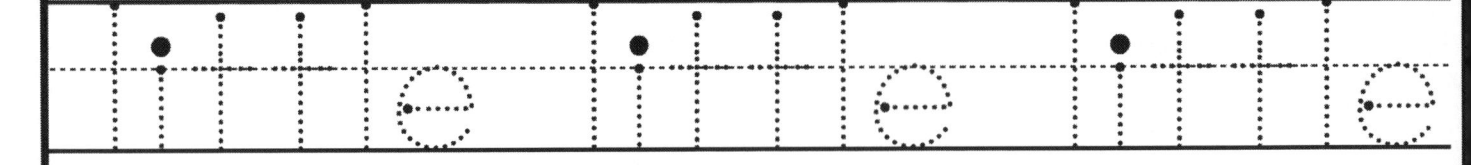

Trace:
little little little

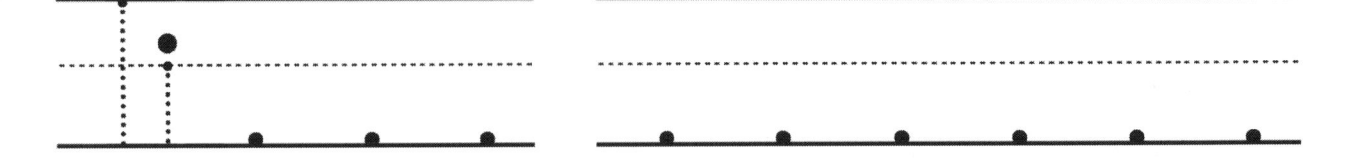

Write:
l

little

Read:

This ball is little.

Circle:

This ball is little.

Trace:

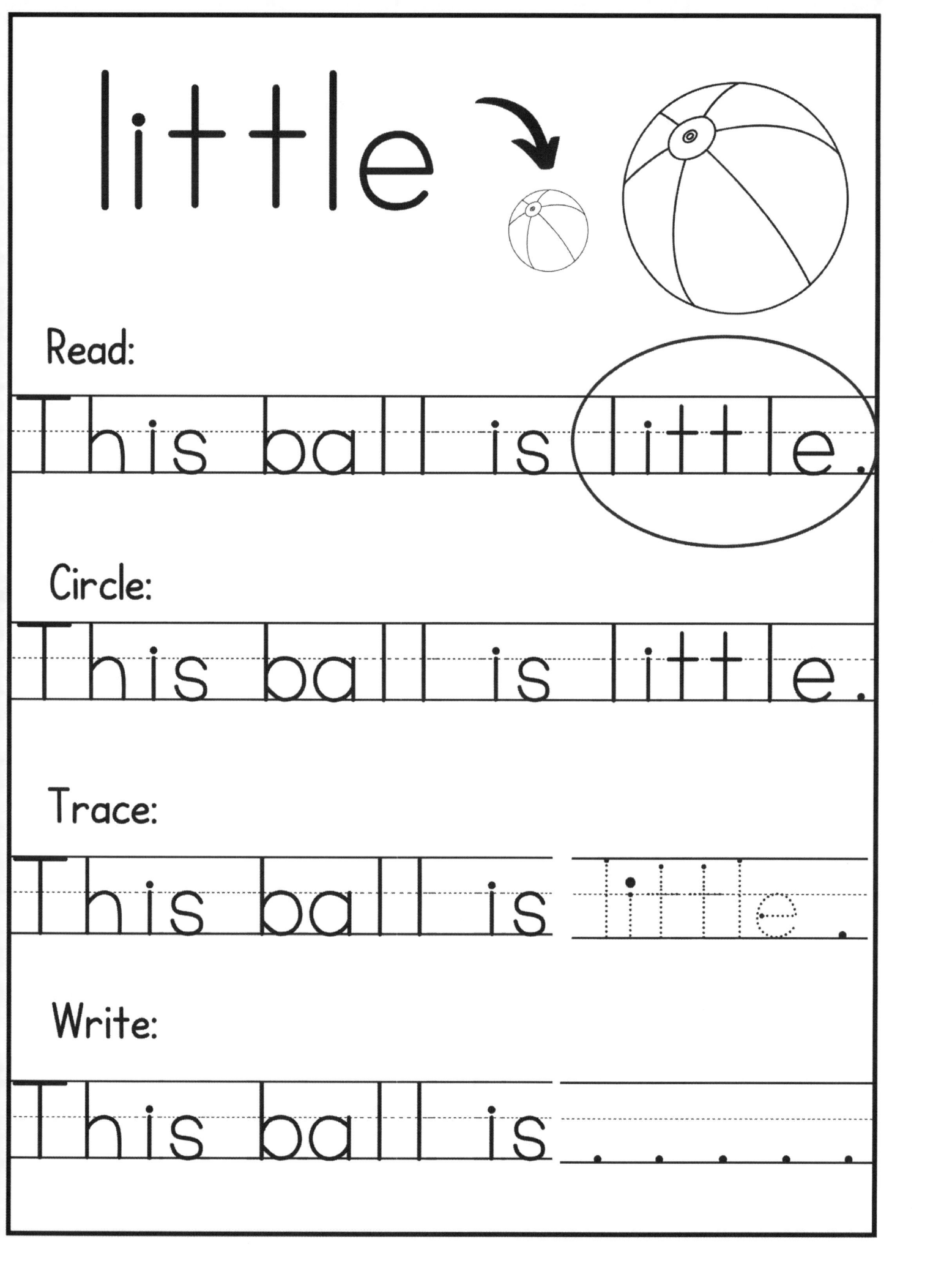

This ball is little.

Write:

This ball is _ _ _ _ _ _.

Review 6

Words learned:

said where away little

Trace the words:

said where away little

Write the words:

s___ w____ a___ l____

Find the words:

said
where
away
little

C W Q A R T
W H X W W I
W E S A I D
B R N Y C Z
E E T V Y B
L I T T L E

Review 6

Circle the sight words in the sentences and trace the sentences:

said where away little

The boy said hi.

Where did you go?

I said go away.

The ball is little.

Say the letters and color: **jump**

Read and Circle:

jump jump jump

Trace:

jump jump jump

Write:

ju j

jump

Read:

I can jump high.

Circle:

I can jump high.

Trace:

I can jump high.

Write:

I can _____ high.

Say the letters and color: **not**

Read and Circle:

not not not

Trace:

not not not

Write:

no n

not

Read:

Do (not) walk there.

Circle:

Do not walk there.

Trace:

Do not walk there.

Write:

Do _ _ _ walk there.

Say the letters and color:

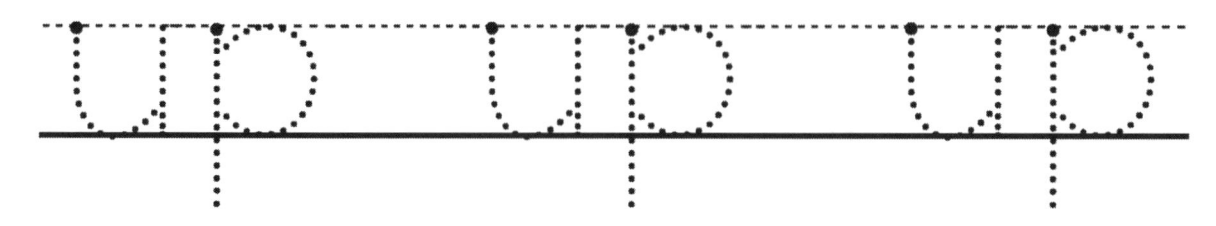

up

Read and Circle:

up up up

Trace:

up up up

Write:

u

up

Read:

The sky is (up).

Circle:

The sky is up.

Trace:

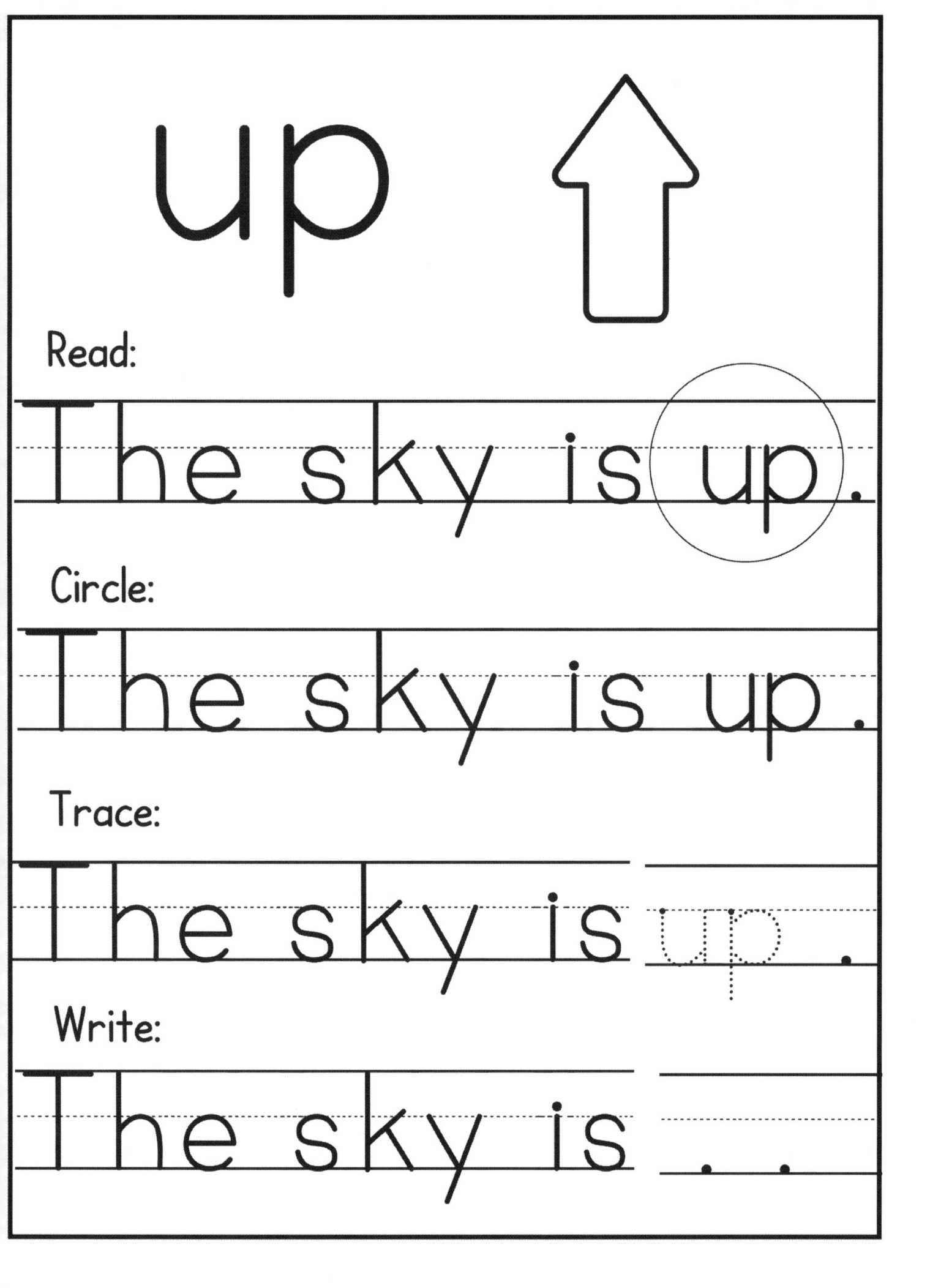

The sky is up.

Write:

The sky is ___ .

Say the letters and color: **play**

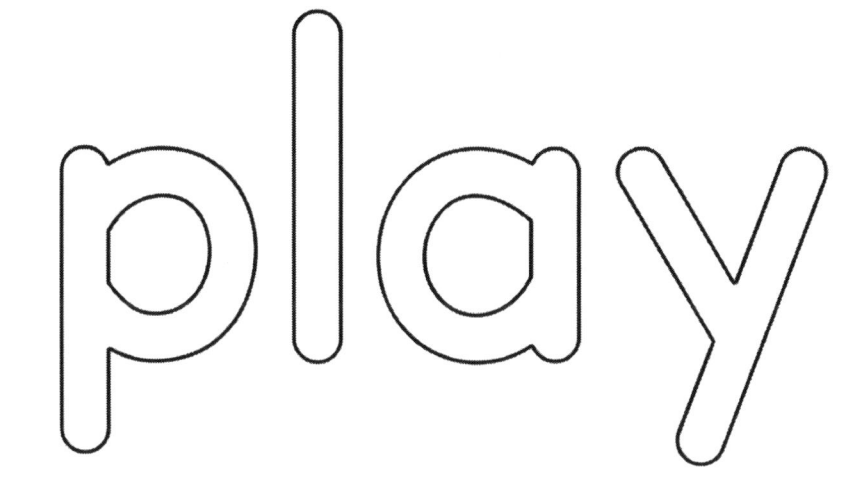

Read and Circle:

play play play

Trace:

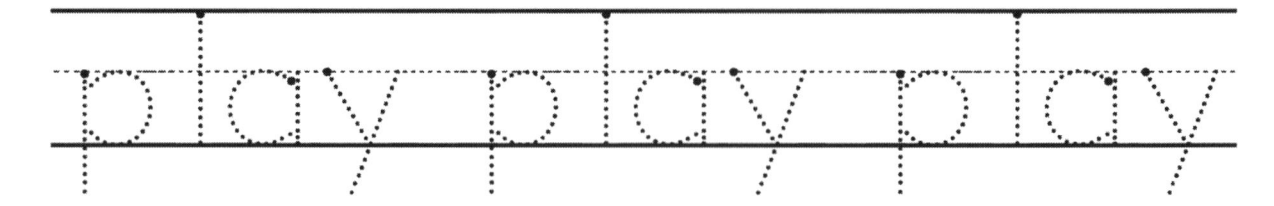

play play play

Write:

p p

play

Read:

I like to play.

Circle:

I like to play.

Trace:

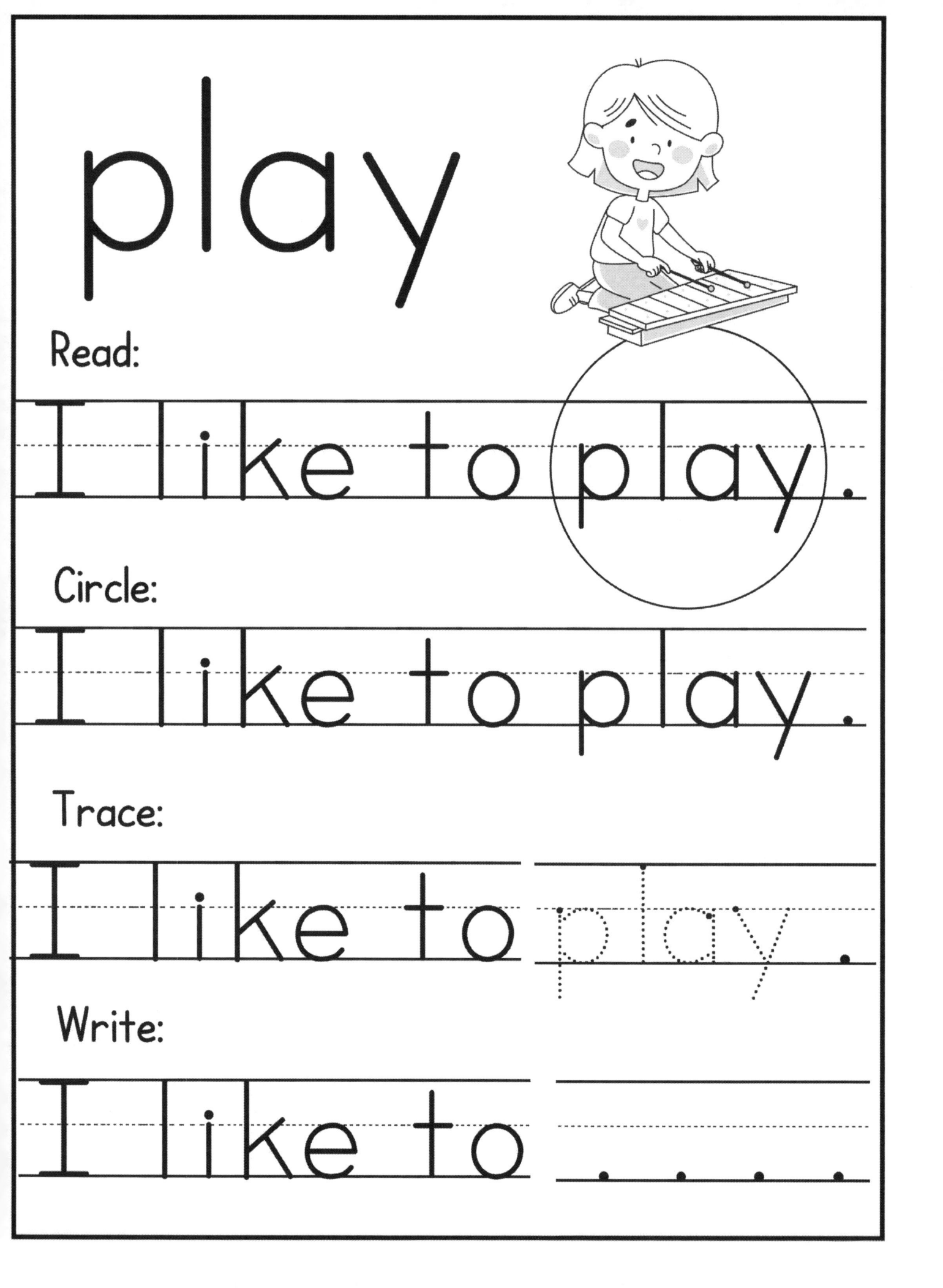

I like to play.

Write:

I like to _____.

Review 7

Words learned:

jump not up play

Trace the words:

jump not up play

Write the words:

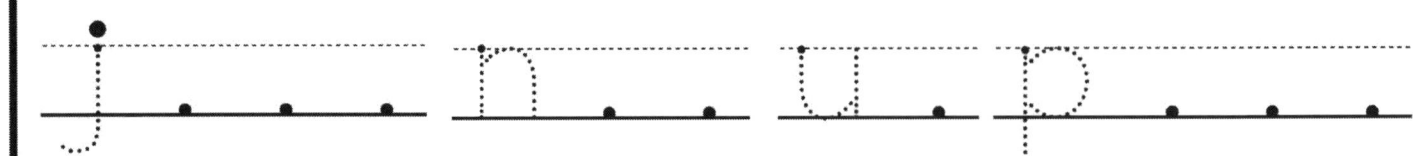

j.... n.. u. p....

Find the words:

jump
not
up
play

P	L	A	Y	X
K	F	A	T	G
J	U	M	P	S
U	N	O	T	B
K	P	L	M	U

Review 7

Circle the sight words in the sentences and trace the sentences:

jump not up play

I can jump high.

Do not walk there.

The sky is up.

I like to play.

Say the letters and color: make

Read and Circle:
make make make

Trace:
make make make

Write:
ma   m

make

Read:

Let`s make lunch.

Circle:

Let`s make lunch.

Trace:

Let`s make lunch.

Write:

Let`s make lunch.

Say the letters and color:

me

Read and Circle:

me me me

Trace:

me me me

Write:

m

me

Read:

This is for (me).

Circle:

This is for me.

Trace:

This is for me.

Write:

This is for ___ .

Say the letters and color:

funny

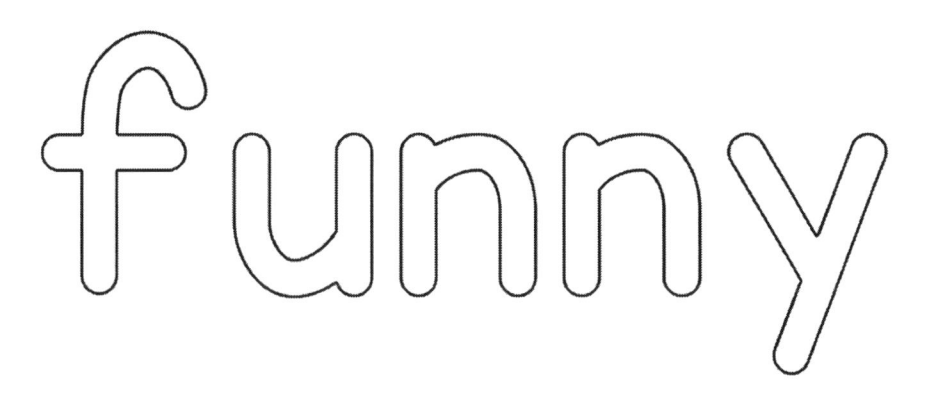

Read and Circle:

funny funny

Trace:

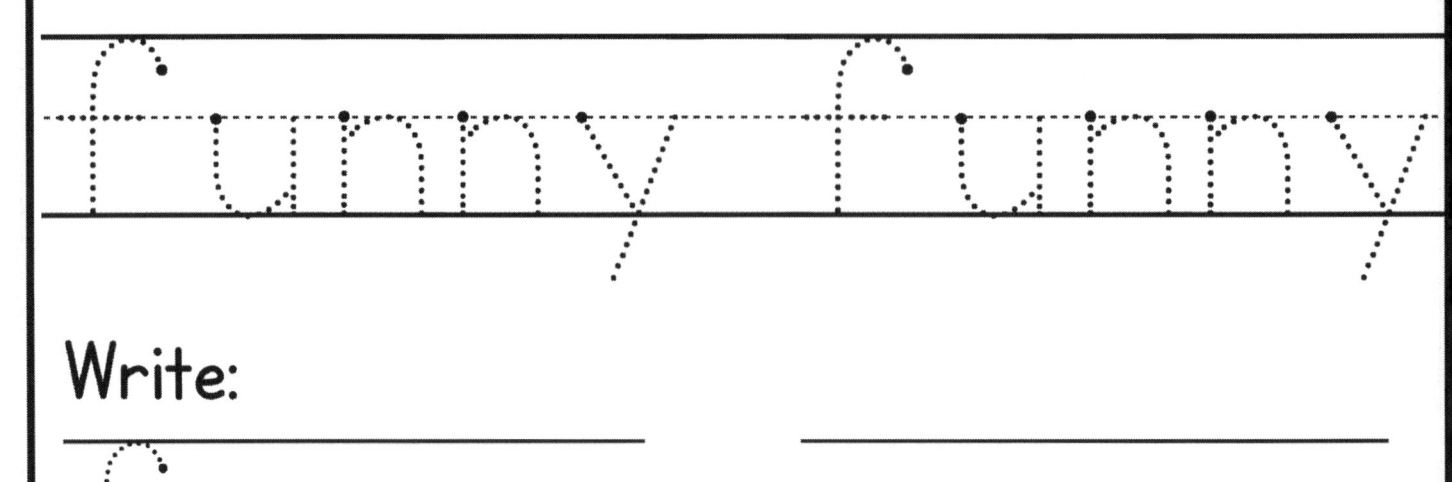

funny funny

Write:

fu

funny

Read:

This joke is (funny).

Circle:

This joke is funny.

Trace:

This joke is funny.

Write:

This joke is _____.

Say the letters and color:

to

Read and Circle:

to to to

Trace:

Write:

to

Read:

I go (to) school.

Circle:

I go to school.

Trace:

I go to school.

Write:

I go . . . school.

Review 8

Words learned:

make me funny to

Trace the words:

make me funny to

Write the words:

m____ m_ f_____ t_

Find the words:

| make |
| me |
| funny |
| to |

A	M	A	K	E
R	T	E	K	U
F	H	D	T	O
F	U	N	N	Y
V	Y	D	U	V

Review 8

Circle the sight words in the sentences and trace the sentences:

make me funny to

Let's make lunch.

This is for me.

This is funny.

I go to school.

Say the letters and color: **one**

Read and Circle:

one one one

Trace:

one one one

Write:

on o

one 1

Read:

I have one nose.

Circle:

I have one nose.

Trace:

I have one nose.

Write:

I have one nose.

Say the letters and color: **two**

Read and Circle:

two two two

Trace:

two two two

Write:

tw t

two 2

Read:

I have (two) legs.

Circle:

I have two legs.

Trace:

I have two legs.

Write:

I have two legs.

Say the letters and color:

three

Read and Circle:

three three

Trace:

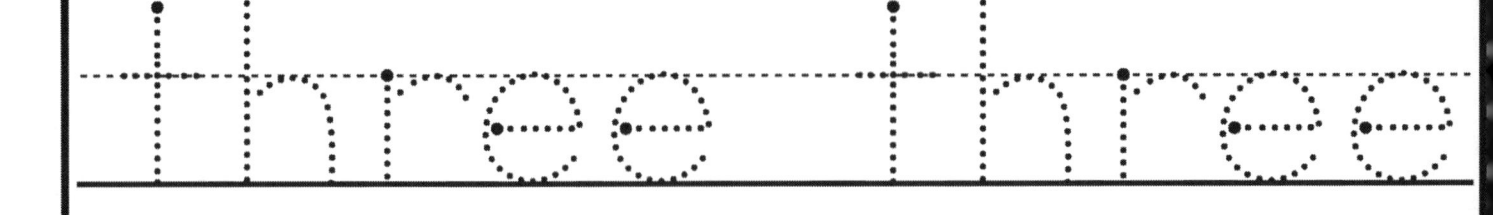

three three

Write:

th

three 3

Read:

I see (three) toys.

Circle:

I see three toys.

Trace:

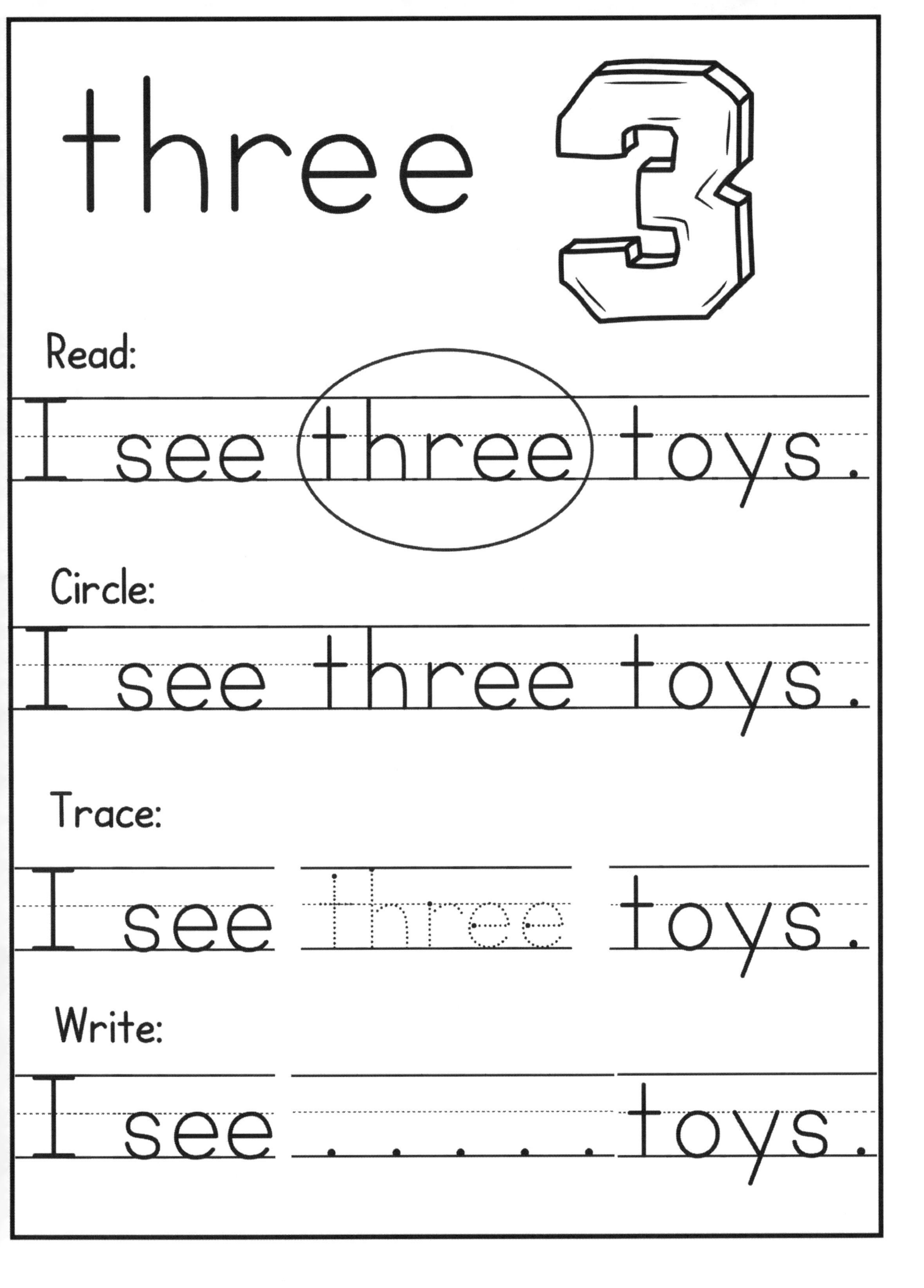

I see three toys.

Write:

I see .... toys.

Review 9

Words learned:

one two three

Trace the words:

one two three

Write the words:

o t t

Find the words:

one
two
three

I Q T K I
O G H T H
Z N R W P
N F E O X
Y Z E T J

Review 9

Circle the sight words in the sentences and trace the sentences:

one two three

I have one nose.

I have two legs.

I see three toys.

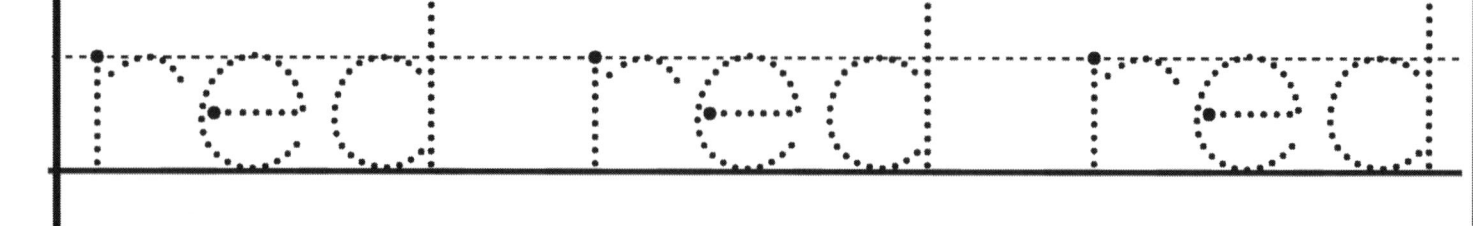

Say the letters and color: **red**

Read and Circle:

red red red

Trace:

red red red

Write:

re r

red

Read:

The apple is red.

Circle:

The apple is red.

Trace:

The apple is red.

Write:

The apple is red.

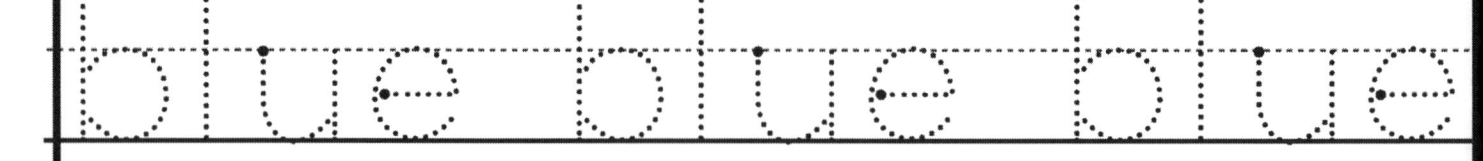

Say the letters and color: **blue**

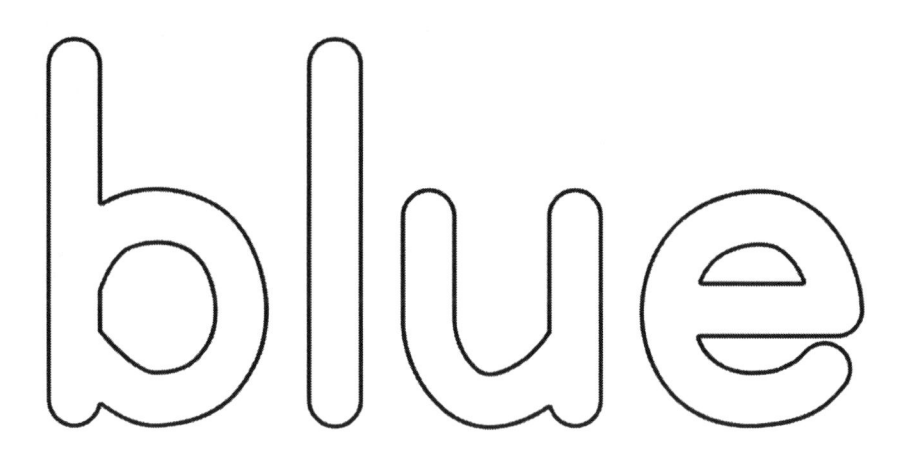

Read and Circle:

blue blue blue

Trace:

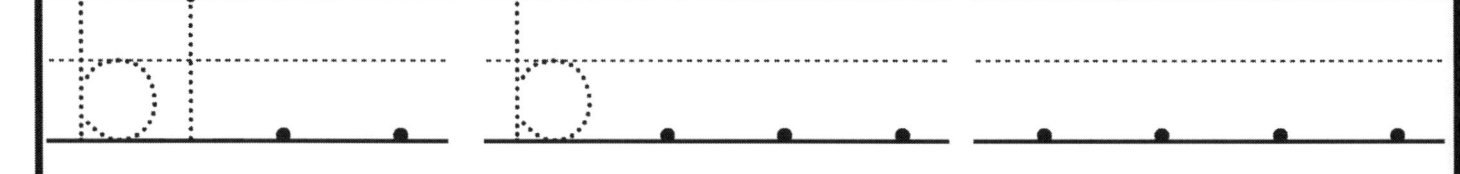

blue blue blue

Write:

b b

blue

Read:

The sky is blue.

Circle:

The sky is blue.

Trace:

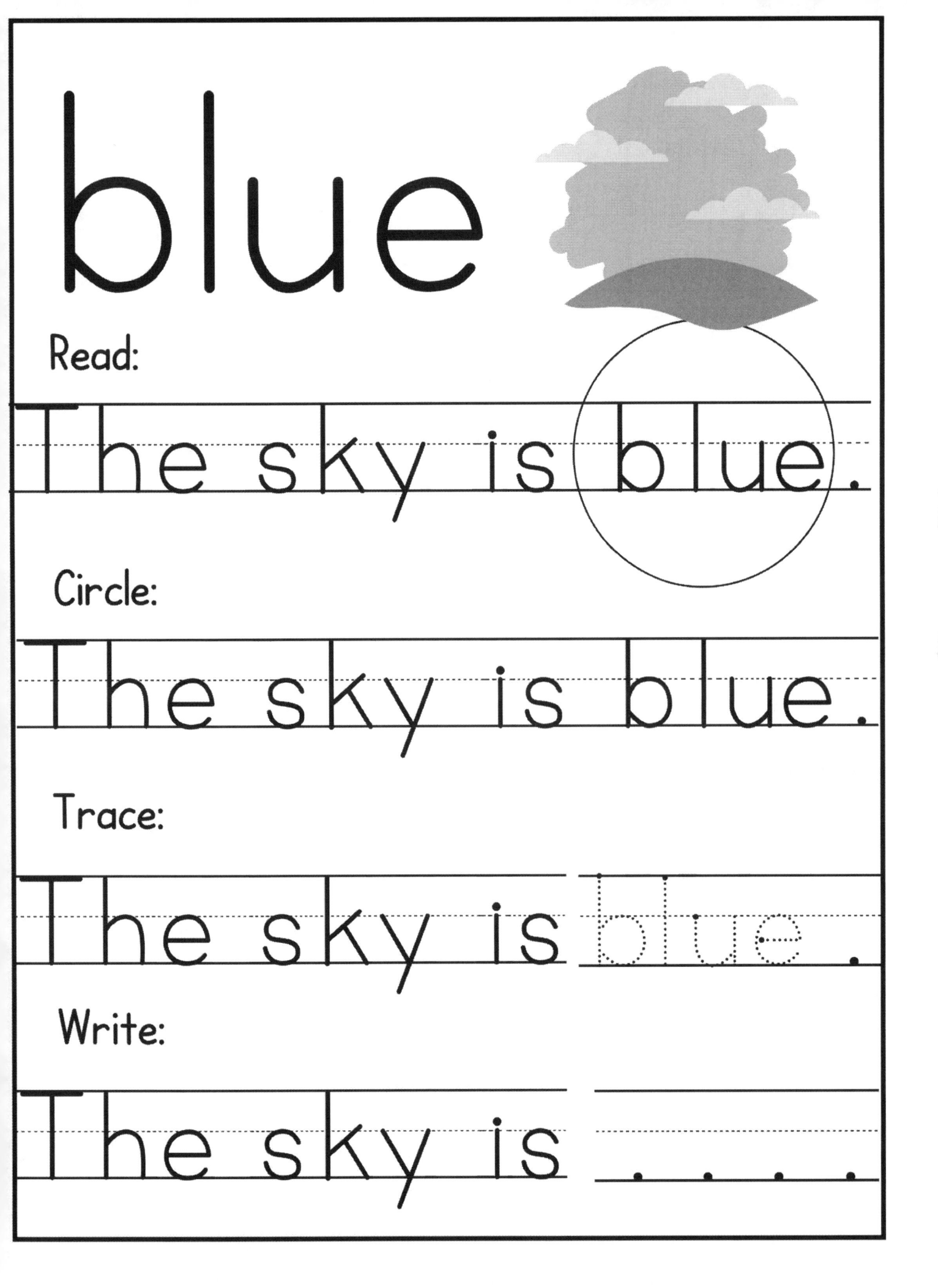

The sky is blue.

Write:

The sky is _____.

Say the letters and color: yellow

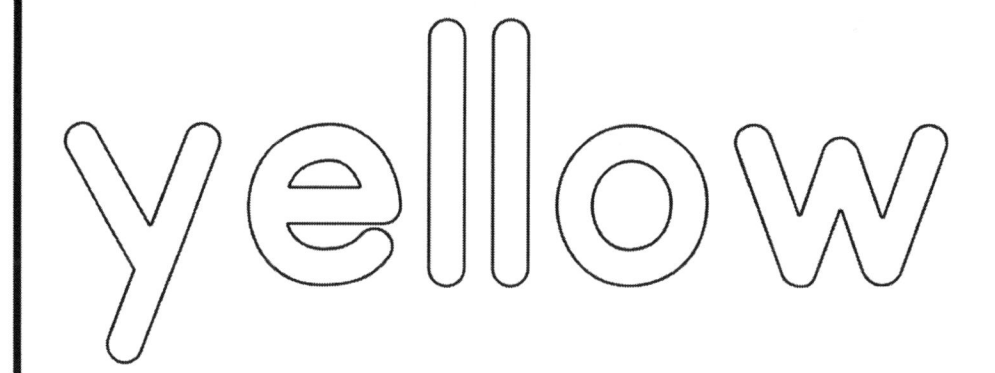

Read and Circle:
yellow yellow

Trace:
yellow yellow

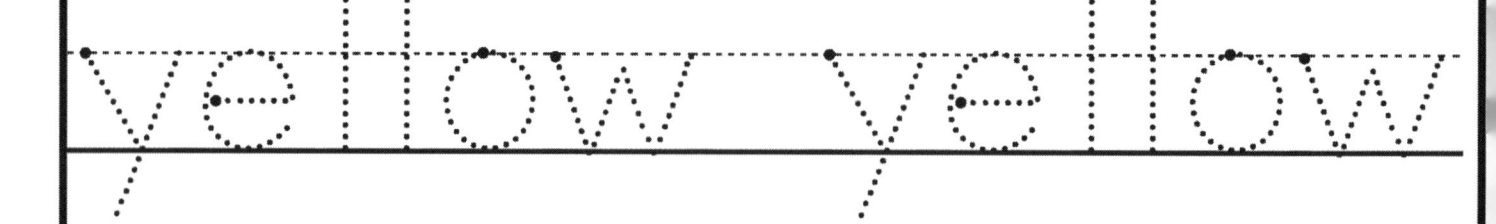

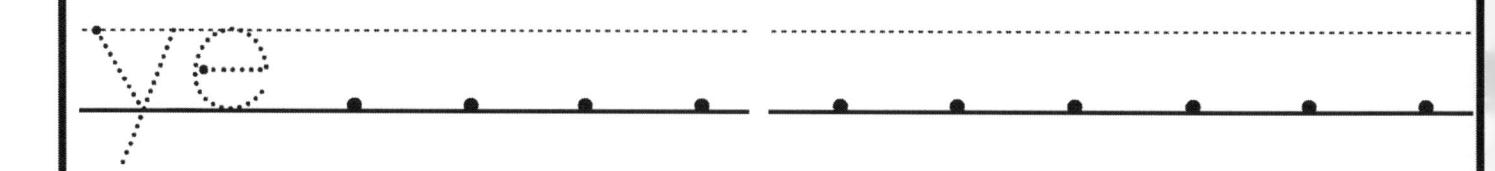

Write:
ye

yellow

Read:

The sun is (yellow.)

Circle:

The sun is yellow.

Trace:

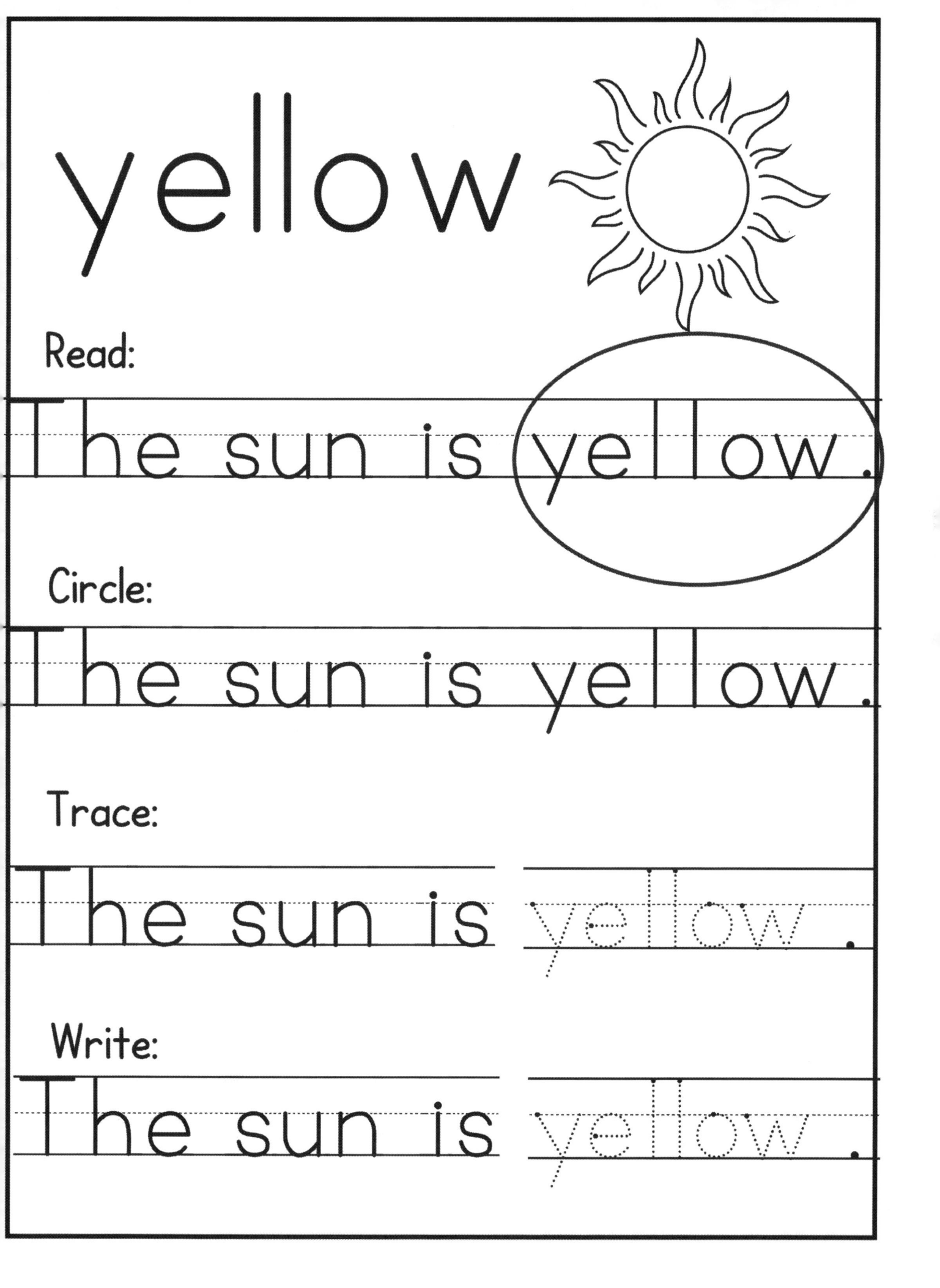

The sun is yellow.

Write:

The sun is yellow.

Review 10

Words learned:

red blue yellow

Trace the words:

red blue yellow

Write the words:

r   b   y

Find the words:

red
blue
yellow

E	J	R	V	R	Y
G	B	Y	Y	E	E
U	V	L	X	D	L
U	N	L	U	Z	L
G	K	W	Y	E	O
O	P	S	R	X	W

Review 10

Circle the sight words in the sentences and trace the sentences:

red blue yellow

The apple is red.

The sky is blue.

The sun is yellow.

Thank You!

Thank you for purchasing this book and we hope you and your little one enjoyed it.

Please check out our website for other educational books from Eventful Minds Publishing.

www.eventfulmindspublishing.com

Made in the USA
Columbia, SC
13 October 2023